Just for the Middle L

- Test Prep Works materials are developed for a specific test and level, making it easier for students to focus on relevant content

- The Middle Level ISEE is for students applying for admission to grades 7-8 – see table at the end of this book for materials for other grades

- Two books are available from Test Prep Works to help students prepare for the Middle Level ISEE

Success on the Middle Level ISEE: A Complete Course

- Strategies for each section of the test
- Reading and vocabulary drills
- In-depth math content instruction with practice sets
- 1 full-length practice test

The Best Unofficial Practice Tests for the Middle Level ISEE

- 2 additional full-length practice tests

TEST PREP WORKS, LLC

Are you an educator?

Incorporate materials from Test Prep Works into your test prep program

- Use the materials developed specifically for the test and level your students are taking

- Customize our books to fit your program

  - Choose content modules from any of our books – even from multiple books

  - Add your branding to the cover and title page

  - Greet your students with an introductory message

  - Create custom books with a one-time setup fee[1], then order copies at list price[2] with no minimum quantities

- Volume discounts available for bulk orders of 50+ copies

You provide the expertise – let us provide the materials

Contact *sales@testprepworks.com* for more info

1 - Setup fees start at $199 per title, which includes branding of the cover and title page and a customer-provided introductory message. Additional customization will incur additional setup fees.

2 - The list price for custom books is the same as the list price of the corresponding title available for retail sale. If the content of a book is modified so that it no longer corresponds to a book available for retail sale, then Test Prep Works will set the list price prior to assessing any setup fees.

TEST PREP WORKS, LLC.

THE BEST Unofficial PRACTICE TESTS FOR THE Middle Level ISEE

Christa Abbott, M.Ed.

Published by:
Test Prep Works, LLC
PO Box 100572
Arlington, VA 22210
www.TestPrepWorks.com

For information about purchasing this title in bulk, or for editions with customized covers or content, please contact us at sales@testprepworks.com or (703) 944-6727.

ISEE is a registered trademark of the ERB. They have not endorsed nor are they associated with this book.

Neither the author nor the publisher of this book claims responsibility for the accuracy of this book or the outcome of students who use these materials.

ISBN: 978-1-939090-14-0

Contents

How To Use This Book

The tests in this book will give you an idea of the types of questions you will see, the concepts that are being tested, and the format and timing of the Middle Level ISEE. You will also get a sense of how the scoring works – one point is given for correct answers and nothing is subtracted for incorrect answers.

Try to work through the test in "real conditions" to get a sense of what it feels like to take a test of this length, which may be longer than what you are used to. Be sure to time yourself on each section and stop when the time is up, just like you will have to on test day.

The following chart lays out the general timing of the test:

Section	Time
Verbal Reasoning – 40 questions	20 minutes
Quantitative Reasoning – 37 questions	35 minutes
--- Five-minute break ---	
Reading Comprehension – 36 questions	35 minutes
Mathematics Achievement – 47 questions	40 minutes
--- Five-minute break ---	
Essay	30 minutes

After you complete Practice Test 1, check all of your answers. Figure out WHY you missed the questions that you answered incorrectly. Then, think about what you would do differently BEFORE you start Practice Test 2.

About the Author

Christa Abbott has been a private test prep tutor for more than a decade, helping her students gain admission to some of the top independent schools in the country. She has now used that experience to develop materials that help students prepare for independent school admissions tests. The approaches used in these books are based on the latest research about how students learn, so that preparation can be an effective and efficient use of time. These materials are also written to be developmentally appropriate for the ages of the students taking the tests.

Christa is a graduate of Middlebury College and received her Masters in Education from the University of Virginia, a program nationally recognized for its excellence. She resides in Arlington, VA, with her husband and three children. Christa continues to coach students one-on-one in the Washington, D.C., area as well as students all over the world via the internet. For more information on these services, please visit www.ChristaAbbott.com.

About Test Prep Works, LLC

Test Prep Works, LLC, was founded to provide effective materials for test preparation. Its founder, Christa Abbott, spent years looking for effective materials for the private school entrance exams but came up empty-handed. The books available combined several different tests and while there are overlaps, they are not the same test. Christa found this to be overwhelming for students who were in elementary and middle school and that just didn't seem necessary. Christa developed her own materials to use with students that are specific for each level of the test and are not just adapted from other books. Now, these materials are available to the general public as well as other tutors. Please visit www.TestPrepWorks.com to view a complete array of offerings as well as sign up for a newsletter with recent news and developments in the world of admissions and test preparation.

Answer Sheets

The following pages contain answer sheets for each of the two practice tests. Additional copies can be downloaded at:

www.testprepworks.com/student/download

Practice Test 1

Section 1: Verbal Reasoning

1 (A) (B) (C) (D)	15 (A) (B) (C) (D)	29 (A) (B) (C) (D)
2 (A) (B) (C) (D)	16 (A) (B) (C) (D)	30 (A) (B) (C) (D)
3 (A) (B) (C) (D)	17 (A) (B) (C) (D)	31 (A) (B) (C) (D)
4 (A) (B) (C) (D)	18 (A) (B) (C) (D)	32 (A) (B) (C) (D)
5 (A) (B) (C) (D)	19 (A) (B) (C) (D)	33 (A) (B) (C) (D)
6 (A) (B) (C) (D)	20 (A) (B) (C) (D)	34 (A) (B) (C) (D)
7 (A) (B) (C) (D)	21 (A) (B) (C) (D)	35 (A) (B) (C) (D)
8 (A) (B) (C) (D)	22 (A) (B) (C) (D)	36 (A) (B) (C) (D)
9 (A) (B) (C) (D)	23 (A) (B) (C) (D)	37 (A) (B) (C) (D)
10 (A) (B) (C) (D)	24 (A) (B) (C) (D)	38 (A) (B) (C) (D)
11 (A) (B) (C) (D)	25 (A) (B) (C) (D)	39 (A) (B) (C) (D)
12 (A) (B) (C) (D)	26 (A) (B) (C) (D)	40 (A) (B) (C) (D)
13 (A) (B) (C) (D)	27 (A) (B) (C) (D)	
14 (A) (B) (C) (D)	28 (A) (B) (C) (D)	

Section 2: Quantitative Reasoning

1 (A) (B) (C) (D)	14 (A) (B) (C) (D)	27 (A) (B) (C) (D)
2 (A) (B) (C) (D)	15 (A) (B) (C) (D)	28 (A) (B) (C) (D)
3 (A) (B) (C) (D)	16 (A) (B) (C) (D)	29 (A) (B) (C) (D)
4 (A) (B) (C) (D)	17 (A) (B) (C) (D)	30 (A) (B) (C) (D)
5 (A) (B) (C) (D)	18 (A) (B) (C) (D)	31 (A) (B) (C) (D)
6 (A) (B) (C) (D)	19 (A) (B) (C) (D)	32 (A) (B) (C) (D)
7 (A) (B) (C) (D)	20 (A) (B) (C) (D)	33 (A) (B) (C) (D)
8 (A) (B) (C) (D)	21 (A) (B) (C) (D)	34 (A) (B) (C) (D)
9 (A) (B) (C) (D)	22 (A) (B) (C) (D)	35 (A) (B) (C) (D)
10 (A) (B) (C) (D)	23 (A) (B) (C) (D)	36 (A) (B) (C) (D)
11 (A) (B) (C) (D)	24 (A) (B) (C) (D)	37 (A) (B) (C) (D)
12 (A) (B) (C) (D)	25 (A) (B) (C) (D)	
13 (A) (B) (C) (D)	26 (A) (B) (C) (D)	

Section 3: Reading Comprehension

1	(A) (B) (C) (D)	13	(A) (B) (C) (D)	25	(A) (B) (C) (D)
2	(A) (B) (C) (D)	14	(A) (B) (C) (D)	26	(A) (B) (C) (D)
3	(A) (B) (C) (D)	15	(A) (B) (C) (D)	27	(A) (B) (C) (D)
4	(A) (B) (C) (D)	16	(A) (B) (C) (D)	28	(A) (B) (C) (D)
5	(A) (B) (C) (D)	17	(A) (B) (C) (D)	29	(A) (B) (C) (D)
6	(A) (B) (C) (D)	18	(A) (B) (C) (D)	30	(A) (B) (C) (D)
7	(A) (B) (C) (D)	19	(A) (B) (C) (D)	31	(A) (B) (C) (D)
8	(A) (B) (C) (D)	20	(A) (B) (C) (D)	32	(A) (B) (C) (D)
9	(A) (B) (C) (D)	21	(A) (B) (C) (D)	33	(A) (B) (C) (D)
10	(A) (B) (C) (D)	22	(A) (B) (C) (D)	34	(A) (B) (C) (D)
11	(A) (B) (C) (D)	23	(A) (B) (C) (D)	35	(A) (B) (C) (D)
12	(A) (B) (C) (D)	24	(A) (B) (C) (D)	36	(A) (B) (C) (D)

Section 4: Mathematics Achievement

1	(A) (B) (C) (D)	17	(A) (B) (C) (D)	33	(A) (B) (C) (D)
2	(A) (B) (C) (D)	18	(A) (B) (C) (D)	34	(A) (B) (C) (D)
3	(A) (B) (C) (D)	19	(A) (B) (C) (D)	35	(A) (B) (C) (D)
4	(A) (B) (C) (D)	20	(A) (B) (C) (D)	36	(A) (B) (C) (D)
5	(A) (B) (C) (D)	21	(A) (B) (C) (D)	37	(A) (B) (C) (D)
6	(A) (B) (C) (D)	22	(A) (B) (C) (D)	38	(A) (B) (C) (D)
7	(A) (B) (C) (D)	23	(A) (B) (C) (D)	39	(A) (B) (C) (D)
8	(A) (B) (C) (D)	24	(A) (B) (C) (D)	40	(A) (B) (C) (D)
9	(A) (B) (C) (D)	25	(A) (B) (C) (D)	41	(A) (B) (C) (D)
10	(A) (B) (C) (D)	26	(A) (B) (C) (D)	42	(A) (B) (C) (D)
11	(A) (B) (C) (D)	27	(A) (B) (C) (D)	43	(A) (B) (C) (D)
12	(A) (B) (C) (D)	28	(A) (B) (C) (D)	44	(A) (B) (C) (D)
13	(A) (B) (C) (D)	29	(A) (B) (C) (D)	45	(A) (B) (C) (D)
14	(A) (B) (C) (D)	30	(A) (B) (C) (D)	46	(A) (B) (C) (D)
15	(A) (B) (C) (D)	31	(A) (B) (C) (D)	47	(A) (B) (C) (D)
16	(A) (B) (C) (D)	32	(A) (B) (C) (D)		

Write your essay topic below

_____

_____

_____

Write your essay below and on the next page

_____

_____

_____

_____

_____

_____

_____

_____

_____

_____

_____

_____

_____

_____

_____

_____

_____

_____

_____

_____

_____

_____

_____

_____

Student Name: _____ Grade Applying For: _____

Use pencil to fill in your answers below.

Practice Test 2

Section 1: Verbal Reasoning

1 (A) (B) (C) (D)	15 (A) (B) (C) (D)	29 (A) (B) (C) (D)
2 (A) (B) (C) (D)	16 (A) (B) (C) (D)	30 (A) (B) (C) (D)
3 (A) (B) (C) (D)	17 (A) (B) (C) (D)	31 (A) (B) (C) (D)
4 (A) (B) (C) (D)	18 (A) (B) (C) (D)	32 (A) (B) (C) (D)
5 (A) (B) (C) (D)	19 (A) (B) (C) (D)	33 (A) (B) (C) (D)
6 (A) (B) (C) (D)	20 (A) (B) (C) (D)	34 (A) (B) (C) (D)
7 (A) (B) (C) (D)	21 (A) (B) (C) (D)	35 (A) (B) (C) (D)
8 (A) (B) (C) (D)	22 (A) (B) (C) (D)	36 (A) (B) (C) (D)
9 (A) (B) (C) (D)	23 (A) (B) (C) (D)	37 (A) (B) (C) (D)
10 (A) (B) (C) (D)	24 (A) (B) (C) (D)	38 (A) (B) (C) (D)
11 (A) (B) (C) (D)	25 (A) (B) (C) (D)	39 (A) (B) (C) (D)
12 (A) (B) (C) (D)	26 (A) (B) (C) (D)	40 (A) (B) (C) (D)
13 (A) (B) (C) (D)	27 (A) (B) (C) (D)	
14 (A) (B) (C) (D)	28 (A) (B) (C) (D)	

Section 2: Quantitative Reasoning

1 (A) (B) (C) (D)	14 (A) (B) (C) (D)	27 (A) (B) (C) (D)
2 (A) (B) (C) (D)	15 (A) (B) (C) (D)	28 (A) (B) (C) (D)
3 (A) (B) (C) (D)	16 (A) (B) (C) (D)	29 (A) (B) (C) (D)
4 (A) (B) (C) (D)	17 (A) (B) (C) (D)	30 (A) (B) (C) (D)
5 (A) (B) (C) (D)	18 (A) (B) (C) (D)	31 (A) (B) (C) (D)
6 (A) (B) (C) (D)	19 (A) (B) (C) (D)	32 (A) (B) (C) (D)
7 (A) (B) (C) (D)	20 (A) (B) (C) (D)	33 (A) (B) (C) (D)
8 (A) (B) (C) (D)	21 (A) (B) (C) (D)	34 (A) (B) (C) (D)
9 (A) (B) (C) (D)	22 (A) (B) (C) (D)	35 (A) (B) (C) (D)
10 (A) (B) (C) (D)	23 (A) (B) (C) (D)	36 (A) (B) (C) (D)
11 (A) (B) (C) (D)	24 (A) (B) (C) (D)	37 (A) (B) (C) (D)
12 (A) (B) (C) (D)	25 (A) (B) (C) (D)	
13 (A) (B) (C) (D)	26 (A) (B) (C) (D)	

Section 3: Reading Comprehension

1	(A) (B) (C) (D)	13	(A) (B) (C) (D)	25	(A) (B) (C) (D)
2	(A) (B) (C) (D)	14	(A) (B) (C) (D)	26	(A) (B) (C) (D)
3	(A) (B) (C) (D)	15	(A) (B) (C) (D)	27	(A) (B) (C) (D)
4	(A) (B) (C) (D)	16	(A) (B) (C) (D)	28	(A) (B) (C) (D)
5	(A) (B) (C) (D)	17	(A) (B) (C) (D)	29	(A) (B) (C) (D)
6	(A) (B) (C) (D)	18	(A) (B) (C) (D)	30	(A) (B) (C) (D)
7	(A) (B) (C) (D)	19	(A) (B) (C) (D)	31	(A) (B) (C) (D)
8	(A) (B) (C) (D)	20	(A) (B) (C) (D)	32	(A) (B) (C) (D)
9	(A) (B) (C) (D)	21	(A) (B) (C) (D)	33	(A) (B) (C) (D)
10	(A) (B) (C) (D)	22	(A) (B) (C) (D)	34	(A) (B) (C) (D)
11	(A) (B) (C) (D)	23	(A) (B) (C) (D)	35	(A) (B) (C) (D)
12	(A) (B) (C) (D)	24	(A) (B) (C) (D)	36	(A) (B) (C) (D)

Section 4: Mathematics Achievement

1	(A) (B) (C) (D)	17	(A) (B) (C) (D)	33	(A) (B) (C) (D)
2	(A) (B) (C) (D)	18	(A) (B) (C) (D)	34	(A) (B) (C) (D)
3	(A) (B) (C) (D)	19	(A) (B) (C) (D)	35	(A) (B) (C) (D)
4	(A) (B) (C) (D)	20	(A) (B) (C) (D)	36	(A) (B) (C) (D)
5	(A) (B) (C) (D)	21	(A) (B) (C) (D)	37	(A) (B) (C) (D)
6	(A) (B) (C) (D)	22	(A) (B) (C) (D)	38	(A) (B) (C) (D)
7	(A) (B) (C) (D)	23	(A) (B) (C) (D)	39	(A) (B) (C) (D)
8	(A) (B) (C) (D)	24	(A) (B) (C) (D)	40	(A) (B) (C) (D)
9	(A) (B) (C) (D)	25	(A) (B) (C) (D)	41	(A) (B) (C) (D)
10	(A) (B) (C) (D)	26	(A) (B) (C) (D)	42	(A) (B) (C) (D)
11	(A) (B) (C) (D)	27	(A) (B) (C) (D)	43	(A) (B) (C) (D)
12	(A) (B) (C) (D)	28	(A) (B) (C) (D)	44	(A) (B) (C) (D)
13	(A) (B) (C) (D)	29	(A) (B) (C) (D)	45	(A) (B) (C) (D)
14	(A) (B) (C) (D)	30	(A) (B) (C) (D)	46	(A) (B) (C) (D)
15	(A) (B) (C) (D)	31	(A) (B) (C) (D)	47	(A) (B) (C) (D)
16	(A) (B) (C) (D)	32	(A) (B) (C) (D)		

Student Name: _____ Grade Applying For: _____

Write in blue or black pen for this essay

Write your essay topic below

_____
_____
_____

Write your essay below and on the next page

_____
_____
_____
_____
_____
_____
_____
_____
_____
_____
_____
_____
_____
_____
_____
_____
_____
_____
_____
_____

Practice Test 1

Verbal Reasoning

40 questions
20 minutes

The Verbal Reasoning section has two parts. When you finish Part One, be sure to keep working on Part Two. For each answer that you choose, make sure to fill in the corresponding circle on the answer sheet.

Part One – Synonyms

The questions in Part One each have a word in all capital letters with four answer choices after it. Choose the answer choice with the word that comes closest in meaning to the word in all capital letters.

SAMPLE QUESTION:

1. SPEEDY:

    (A) loud
    (B) messy
    ● quick
    (D) small

Part Two – Sentence Completions

The questions in Part Two each have a sentence with one blank. The blank takes the place of a word that is missing. The sentence has four answer choices after it. Choose the answer choice that would best complete the meaning of the sentence.

SAMPLE QUESTION:

1. Since the weather is getting warmer every day, it is particularly important to -------- more water.

    (A) create
    ● drink
    (C) leave
    (D) waste

STOP

DO NOT MOVE ON TO THE SECTION UNTIL TOLD TO

Part One - Synonyms

Directions: Choose the word that is closest in meaning to the word that is in all capital letters.

1. WRETCHED:

   (A) attentive
   (B) formidable
   (C) miserable
   (D) saintly

2. DWELL:

   (A) contain
   (B) live
   (C) pity
   (D) tailor

3. LULL:

   (A) calm
   (B) entice
   (C) peel
   (D) sanction

4. SNUG:

   (A) kindred
   (B) lame
   (C) mediocre
   (D) tight

5. PERPETUAL:

   (A) distant
   (B) endless
   (C) general
   (D) ridiculous

6. CRITICAL:

   (A) distinct
   (B) fluid
   (C) important
   (D) thrilling

7. CREED:

   (A) beliefs
   (B) embarrassment
   (C) jealousy
   (D) treaty

8. OBSOLETE:

   (A) civilized
   (B) earnest
   (C) old
   (D) remarkable

9. BRAWN:

   (A) bulge
   (B) interruption
   (C) label
   (D) strength

10. RECEDE:

   (A) remain
   (B) remote
   (C) reserve
   (D) retreat

CONTINUE TO THE NEXT PAGE

11. PROBABLE:

   (A) fragrant
   (B) likely
   (C) jagged
   (D) rapid

12. SWIVEL:

   (A) amplify
   (B) deduct
   (C) spin
   (D) tolerate

13. EMBRACE:

   (A) contact
   (B) ditch
   (C) preach
   (D) welcome

14. EVIDENT:

   (A) obvious
   (B) prompt
   (C) radiant
   (D) tedious

15. TARNISH:

   (A) prevail
   (B) stain
   (C) toil
   (D) warm

16. HAUGHTY:

   (A) appealing
   (B) faithful
   (C) snobbish
   (D) taken

17. SPLENDID:

   (A) grand
   (B) powerful
   (C) relieved
   (D) urgent

18. DUPE:

   (A) fool
   (B) haul
   (C) pack
   (D) spread

19. MEAGER:

   (A) crooked
   (B) definite
   (C) skimpy
   (D) temporary

20. CONCISE:

   (A) ambitious
   (B) brief
   (C) lavish
   (D) rescued

CONTINUE TO THE NEXT PAGE

Part Two – Sentence Completions

Directions: Choose the word to best complete the sentence.

21. After years of neglect, it wasn't enough to fix just parts of Grand Central Station, rather the entire building needed a major --------.

    (A) accomplice
    (B) equivalent
    (C) interrogation
    (D) overhaul

22. Although Coco Chanel came from very humble origins, her wealth and influence came to ------- that of people born to some of the most powerful families in Europe.

    (A) flatter
    (B) grieve
    (C) rival
    (D) value

23. In the short story "The Tell-Tale Heart", Edgar Allan Poe uses an eerie sounding clock in order to create a sense of -------- and doom.

    (A) foreboding
    (B) logic
    (C) motion
    (D) respect

24. Bonnie Parker became one of the most famous --------- of all time after she went with Clyde Barrow to rob several banks.

    (A) accomplices
    (B) criticisms
    (C) rulers
    (D) specifications

CONTINUE TO THE NEXT PAGE

25. The Pulitzer Prize is an award given to very few people and therefore carries with it a lot of ----------.

   (A) flaws
   (B) prestige
   (C) secrecy
   (D) tokens

26. Rather than offering their full menu of food, many restaurants offer only a -------- menu for catering events.

   (A) complete
   (B) delicious
   (C) lavish
   (D) partial

27. Before beans can be cooked, they needed to be sorted --------- for small stones since even a tiny fragment of stone could chip a tooth of the person who will eventually eat the beans.

   (A) lazily
   (B) nearly
   (C) thoroughly
   (D) warmly

28. During the California gold rush, many -------- quickly set up shop in mining towns in order to sell food and supplies to the people who came to find their fortunes.

   (A) doctors
   (B) lawyers
   (C) proprietors
   (D) treasurers

CONTINUE TO THE NEXT PAGE

29. The corrosive salt air in seaside locations means that buildings quickly become -------
    if they are not actively maintained.

    (A) decrepit
    (B) frivolous
    (C) horticulture
    (D) nimble

30. The butterfly effect theory suggests that even a(n) -------- change, such as a butterfly
    flapping its wings, can lead to major events down the road in a distant place.

    (A) earnest
    (B) immense
    (C) jubilant
    (D) slight

31. Journalists Bob Woodward and Carl Bernstein had to -------- a huge amount of
    evidence before they could accuse the sitting United States president, Richard Nixon,
    of illegal activities.

    (A) avoid
    (B) compile
    (C) diminish
    (D) fray

32. In contrast to the impassioned protesters outside the palace walls, the Queen of
    France Marie Antoinette is said to have had a ---------- attitude about the starving
    citizens of France.

    (A) classic
    (B) flickering
    (C) nonchalant
    (D) sensitive

CONTINUE TO THE NEXT PAGE

33. In the early 1900s, choreographer Sergei Diaghilev and composer Igor Stravinsky created a ballet that was such a -------- change from previous ballets that the audience rioted when it was performed.

(A) drastic
(B) familiar
(C) genteel
(D) sullen

34. Oil and water are known for not ------- since if they are placed in a clear container it is easy to see that the two do not mix.

(A) burning
(B) dominating
(C) intermingling
(D) receding

35. When Copernicus suggested that the earth rotated around the sun, religious officials tried to -------- this idea even though Copernicus was correct.

(A) define
(B) elevate
(C) pluck
(D) suppress

36. When the first moving pictures were first created in the 1890s audiences were absolutely ------- by the photographs that moved realistically, which was the beginning of a fascination with cinema.

(A) bored
(B) captivated
(C) isolated
(D) restrained

CONTINUE TO THE NEXT PAGE

37. Before computers were introduced, secretaries often wrote in ------- words because it would take too long to write down complete words as a person spoke.

    (A) abbreviated
    (B) educated
    (C) mammoth
    (D) picturesque

38. Although is often assumed that politicians from opposing political parties ------ one another, after the election is over they often work and socialize together.

    (A) convince
    (B) ignore
    (C) loathe
    (D) respect

39. Millions of Americans watched the ------- of the spacecraft Apollo 11 when its launch was televised on July 16, 1969.

    (A) building
    (B) commission
    (C) equality
    (D) trajectory

40. In 1918, the national anthem went from being a song occasionally sung at games to being a(n) ------- part of every American baseball game.

    (A) aloof
    (B) integral
    (C) obedient
    (D) unique

STOP

IF YOU HAVE TIME LEFT YOU MAY CHECK YOUR ANSWERS IN THIS SECTION ONLY

Quantitative Reasoning

37 questions

35 minutes

Each math question has four answer choices after it. Choose the answer choice that best answers the question.

Make sure that you fill in the correct answer on your answer sheet. You may write in the test booklet.

SAMPLE QUESTION:

1. What is the perimeter of a rectangle that has a length of 3 cm and a width of 5 cm?

   $(P = 2l + 2w)$

   (A) 6 cm
   (B) 10 cm
   (C) 8 cm
   ● 16 cm

The correct answer is 16 cm and circle D is filled in.

STOP

DO NOT MOVE ON TO THE SECTION UNTIL TOLD TO

Part One – Word Problems

1. Nadine surveyed her neighbors about their ages. The histogram below shows her data.

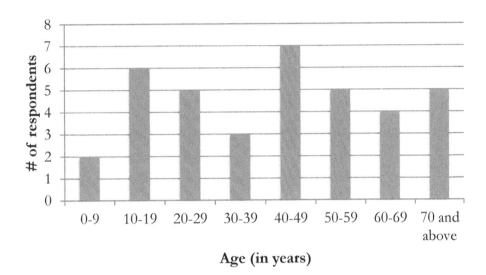

    Which could be the median age of the neighbors that Nadine surveyed?

    (A) 29
    (B) 39
    (C) 43
    (D) 50

2. In Kim's class there are currently four more boys than girls. If there were three more boys in her class, then there would be twice as many boys as girls. How many girls are currently in Kim's class?

    (A) 4
    (B) 7
    (C) 11
    (D) 14

CONTINUE TO THE NEXT PAGE

3. The mean of Stuart's scores on 6 quizzes is 12. If he would like to raise the mean of his quiz scores by 2, what must he score on his 7th quiz?

   (A) 2
   (B) 6
   (C) 18
   (D) 26

4. A restaurant has 8 saltshakers that can each hold 1 cup of salt. There are 3 saltshakers that contain $\frac{1}{3}$ cup of salt and 5 saltshakers that contain $\frac{1}{2}$ cup of salt. How many cups of salt are needed if all of the saltshakers are going to be filled completely?

   (A) 4.5 cups
   (B) 5 cups
   (C) 5.5 cups
   (D) 6.0 cups

5. A bag contains black and white tiles. If 30% of the tiles are black and there are 6 black tiles, then how many of the tiles are white?

   (A) 3
   (B) 14
   (C) 16
   (D) 18

6. The area of the largest triangle below is 72 in^2.

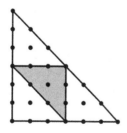

   What is the area of the shaded portion?

   (A) 9 in^2
   (B) 12 in^2
   (C) 18 in^2
   (D) 24 in^2

CONTINUE TO THE NEXT PAGE

7. The square root of 50 is between

   (A) 7 and 8
   (B) 8 and 9
   (C) 9 and 10
   (D) 10 and 11

8. The ratio of the side lengths of two cubes is 1 to 3. What is the ratio of their volumes?

   (A) 1 to 3
   (B) 1 to 6
   (C) 1 to 9
   (D) 1 to 27

9. Joshua is building a scale model of a train. The length of the train on his model is 12 inches and the actual length of the train is 30 feet. If the actual width of the train is 12 feet, how wide should his model train be?

   (A) 1.2 inches
   (B) 2.4 inches
   (C) 3.6 inches
   (D) 4.8 inches

10. The Acela train travels at a speed that is three times the speed of the Downeaster train. If they were to leave the same station at the same time and travel the same route, after 30 minutes the Acela train would 50 miles ahead of the Downeaster. Which equation could be used to find the speed (D) of the Downeaster train in miles per hour?

   (A) $\dfrac{1}{2}D + 50 = \dfrac{3}{2}D$

   (B) $\dfrac{1}{2}D = \dfrac{3}{2}D + 50$

   (C) $30D + 50 = 90D$

   (D) $30D = 90D + 50$

CONTINUE TO THE NEXT PAGE

11. Wilbert had 34 figurines in his collection before his birthday party. His collection increased by 150% at his party. How many figurines does he now have?

   (A) 51
   (B) 85
   (C) 96
   (D) 102

12. There are 4 red marbles and 6 blue marbles in a bag. A marble is to be drawn, then replaced, and then a second marble will be drawn. What is the probability that both marbles will be red?

   (A) $\dfrac{2}{25}$

   (B) $\dfrac{4}{25}$

   (C) $\dfrac{4}{10}$

   (D) $\dfrac{8}{10}$

13. If $9x - 6 = 30$, then what is the value of $3x - 2$?

   (A) 3
   (B) 4
   (C) 10
   (D) 18

CONTINUE TO THE NEXT PAGE

14. The graph below shows how the cost of shipping relates to the number of books ordered.

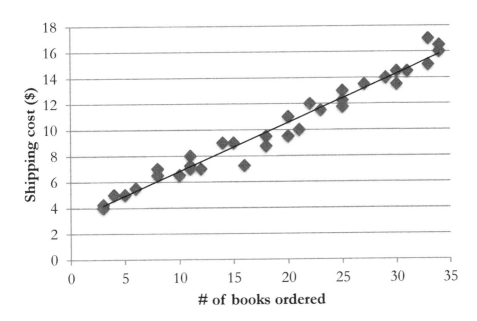

What is the average cost of shipping for a single book if 25 books are ordered? (Use the line of best fit.)

(A) $0.50

(B) $0.75

(C) $6.60

(D) $13.00

CONTINUE TO THE NEXT PAGE

15. The figure below is a net. A net is a two-dimensional representation that can be folded into a three-dimensional object. The figure below is to be cut along the solid lines and folded along the dotted lines.

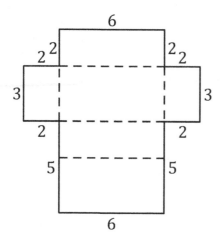

What is the volume of the three dimensional object that would be created by folding this net?

(A) 16 units^3

(B) 24 units^3

(C) 30 units^3

(D) 36 units^3

16. A machine accepts a number as an input and then produces an output. It applies the same rule each time. A few sample inputs/outputs are shown below.

Input	Output
1	1
2	8
3	27

If the machine produced an output of 125, what was the input?

(A) 4

(B) 5

(C) 10

(D) 25

CONTINUE TO THE NEXT PAGE

17. The large cube below was created by stacking smaller cubes.

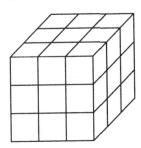

How many smaller cubes were used to make the large cube?

(A) 18
(B) 24
(C) 27
(D) 81

18. Raymond bought four pairs of socks that cost $8 each. There was also 6% sales tax added to his order as well as a shipping fee. If his total cost was $37.92, what was the shipping fee?

(A) $4.00
(B) $4.50
(C) $5.92
(D) $6.00

CONTINUE TO THE NEXT PAGE

19. Which answer choice shows the function for which the *y*-values decrease at the greatest rate as the *x*-values increase?

(A)

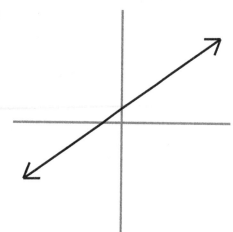

(B)

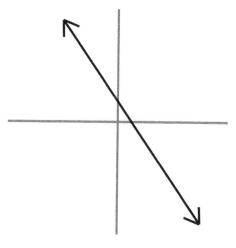

(C)

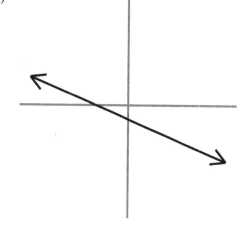

(D)

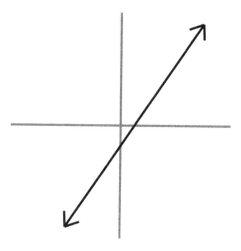

CONTINUE TO THE NEXT PAGE

Part Two — Quantitative Comparisons

Directions: Use the information in the question to compare the quantities in Columns A and B. After comparing the two quantities, choose the correct answer choice:

- (A) Quantity in Column A is greater.
- (B) Quantity in Column B is greater.
- (C) The quantities in Column A and Column B are equal.
- (D) Cannot be determined from the information given.

A t-shirt costs $10 at regular price.

Column A	**Column B**
20. The price of the t-shirt after a 30% discount	The price of the t-shirt after two separate 15% discounts

---

$$7w + 12 = 96$$
$$\frac{v}{3} + 6 = 18$$

Column A	**Column B**
21. w	v

Column A	**Column B**
22. $\sqrt{3.6}$	$\sqrt{0.36}$

Column A	**Column B**
23. -2^3	$(-2)^3$

CONTINUE TO THE NEXT PAGE

	Column A	Column B
24.	The slope between $(3, 2)$ and $(7, 5)$	The slope of $4x + 7y = 5$

Anthony has $1.36 in dimes, nickels, and pennies only.
(Note: 1 dime = $0.10, 1 nickel = $0.05, 1 penny = $0.01)

	Column A	Column B
25.	The least number of coins that Anthony could have	14

Ms. Barker drove for 15 minutes at an average speed of 40 miles per hour.
Ms. Alexander drove for 20 minutes at 30 miles per hour.

	Column A	Column B
26.	Distance that Ms. Barker drove	Distance that Ms. Alexander drove

	Column A	Column B
27.	2	$2 + x$

	Column A	Column B
28.	10% of 765	50% of 153

CONTINUE TO THE NEXT PAGE

	Column A	**Column B**
29.	7	$\sqrt{50}$

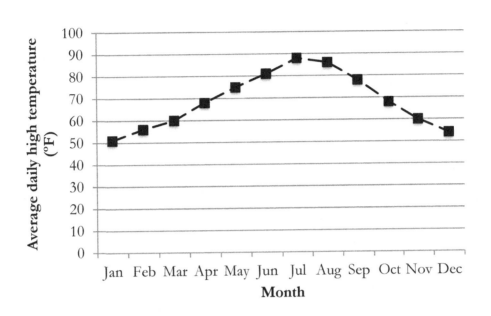

	Column A	**Column B**
30.	Average daily high temperature in February	Average daily high temperature in November

Noel is going to roll two cubes with their faces numbered 1 to 6. The numbers that are shown on the top of each cube will then be added together.

	Column A	**Column B**
31.	The probability that the sum of the two numbers will be greater than 6	The probability that the sum of the two numbers will be less than 6

CONTINUE TO THE NEXT PAGE

x is a number less than 0.

Column A	Column B
$1 + x$	$1 - x$

32.

Column A	Column B
$\dfrac{1}{778}$	$\dfrac{1}{779}$

33.

In a new currency system, 1 harp is equal to 120 lules

Column A	Column B
840 lules	7 harps

34.

Column A	Column B
x^2	x^3

35.

12 packages of gum costs $5.

Column A	Column B
The cost of 5 packages of gum	$2

36.

$$m \leq 0$$
$$n \geq 0$$

Column A	Column B
m	n

37.

STOP

IF YOU HAVE TIME LEFT YOU MAY CHECK YOUR ANSWERS IN THIS SECTION ONLY

Reading Comprehension

36 questions

35 minutes

The Reading Comprehension section has six short passages. Each passage has six questions after it. Choose the answer choice that comes closest to what is stated or implied in the passage. You can write in the test booklet.

STOP

DO NOT MOVE ON TO THE SECTION UNTIL TOLD TO

Questions 1-6

1   It is commonly said that Christopher Columbus' journey to the New World in the
2 1400s was particularly brave since people at that time thought that the earth was flat.
3 There was a danger that ships could sail right off the edge of the earth, or so the story
4 goes. However, there is good evidence that since the time of the ancient Greeks,
5 educated people knew that Earth was in fact a spherical shape.

6   In sixth century B.C.E., Pythagoras suggested that the earth was not flat. He
7 believed that the earth was in fact round and rotated around antipodes, which today we
8 would refer to as the north and south poles. For a few hundred years, the idea of a round
9 earth remained in question. By the time of Plato, around the 3rd century B.C.E.,
10 however, it was widely accepted that the earth existed in the shape of a sphere. Ships
11 often sailed off the edge of the horizon, after all, and returned in one piece.

12   It has also been suggested that the fact that Earth is not flat was forgotten during
13 the Middle Ages. This would explain how ancient Greeks could know that the earth was
14 spherical but Columbus would not have. However, texts from the Middle Ages clearly
15 show that scholars knew that the earth was round. By the 15th century, the time in which
16 Columbus sailed, it would have been unheard of for an educated person to believe that
17 the earth was flat.

18   The idea that people at the time of Columbus would have believed the earth to be
19 flat wasn't even popularized until 1828. At this time, Washington Irving wrote *A*
20 *History of the Life and Voyages of Christopher Columbus*. In this book, Irving created a
21 fictional account of meetings between Columbus and the commission that approved
22 and financed his voyage. In this account, the commission doubted Columbus' assertion
23 that the earth was round for religious reasons. It is ludicrous to believe that the highly
24 educated commission would have believed the earth was flat, however.

25   The commissions' real objection to Columbus' trip was that they did not agree with
26 the distances that Columbus had calculated. Historically, ships sailed east to reach
27 Japan. Columbus calculated that by sailing west, Japan would only be about 5,000 miles
28 from the coast of Portugal. The commission was right to object to these calculations. It
29 turns out that Columbus had underestimated the distance to Japan by about 15,000
30 miles.

31   When Columbus left Portugal, it is highly unlikely that he would have been afraid
32 of sailing off the edge of the earth. Rather, he should have feared that critics were right
33 and he had underestimated the distance to Japan. When Columbus' ships encountered
34 the Caribbean Islands, it was quite a stroke of luck. Columbus' crew had run out of
35 supplies and were near mutiny. It wasn't a flat earth but rather a crew of starving sailors
36 that made Columbus' journey a risky one.

CONTINUE TO THE NEXT PAGE

1. The primary purpose of this passage is to

   (A) explain that Columbus was not a great mathematician.
   (B) describe how a myth began.
   (C) disprove a common misconception.
   (D) suggest that Columbus didn't make it to Japan.

2. Which statement regarding Columbus is best supported with evidence from the passage?

   (A) He feared sailing of the edge of the world.
   (B) His journey was financed by a commission.
   (C) He was trying to sail to the Caribbean Islands.
   (D) He did not return from the Caribbean Islands.

3. It can be inferred from the passage that Columbus was leaving from

   (A) Portugal.
   (B) Japan.
   (C) America.
   (D) the Caribbean Islands.

4. In line 23, the word "ludicrous" comes closest in meaning to

   (A) dismayed.
   (B) festive.
   (C) precise.
   (D) ridiculous.

5. What does the passage imply about Washington Irving?

   (A) He wrote a well-researched account of Columbus' journey.
   (B) He introduced an error into the story of Christopher Columbus.
   (C) He personally knew Christopher Columbus.
   (D) He lived in the 3rd century B.C.E.

6. The purpose of the last paragraph (lines 31-36) is to

   (A) explain the real difficulty that Columbus ran into.
   (B) relate a story about sailors.
   (C) imply that the sailors thought that Earth was flat.
   (D) introduce a new solution to a problem.

CONTINUE TO THE NEXT PAGE

Questions 7-12

1   There are many ways for an animal to perceive what objects surround them.
2 Humans, among others, often rely almost exclusively on their sense of sight in order to
3 assess their environment. Some creatures don't have the benefit of sight to navigate
4 their world, however. Perhaps they fly at night or swim through the deep ocean where
5 there is no light to see by. Some of these animals rely on a different method of
6 discernment called echolocation.

7   In order to use echolocation, animals emit a call. This call travels through the air
8 as soundwaves. These soundwaves bounce off of objects that they encounter and then
9 travel back to the animal. The animal can then use the length of time between emitting
10 the call and perceiving the waves bounced back to determine how far away an object is.
11 Animals can also use these soundwaves to figure out in what direction an object lays.
12 They use the difference between when the sound is perceived by their right ear and left
13 ear to determine direction.

14   One group of animals that utilizes echolocation is microbats. These bats are very
15 small and therefore easy prey for larger animals. Echolocation allows microbats to hunt
16 in almost total darkness, giving the microbats two important advantages. First of all, it
17 allows them to hunt when most other animals cannot see and therefore are not out
18 seeking food. Secondly, many insects come out to feed only when it is very dark. Since
19 insects are the primary food source for microbats, being able to hunt in the conditions
20 in which insects emerge is important.

21   Another group of animals that uses echolocation is toothed whales. This group
22 includes dolphins, porpoises, and killer whales, among others. Echolocation works
23 particularly well for marine animals because sound waves travel well through water
24 while light rays do not. In the murky darkness of the ocean, toothed whales have
25 survived because of their ability to use echolocation to determine the location of prey.

CONTINUE TO THE NEXT PAGE

7. What is the main idea of this passage?

   (A) Bats are the only animals that use echolocation.
   (B) Echolocation is particularly helpful for marine animals.
   (C) Humans are incapable of echolocation.
   (D) Some animals use echolocation to determine their surroundings.

8. It can be inferred from the passage that most animals

   (A) use echolocation.
   (B) are marine animals.
   (C) hunt during the day.
   (D) eat insects.

9. The author implies echolocation is particularly helpful in marine animals because

   (A) animals can't see to hunt prey in the dark ocean.
   (B) light waves travel further than sound waves.
   (C) most animals sleep during the night in the deep ocean.
   (D) there are no natural predators.

10. In line 19, the word "primary" most closely means

   (A) limited.
   (B) main.
   (C) satisfying.
   (D) unimportant.

11. The passage states that the distance to an object can be measured by

   (A) which ear perceives the echo first.
   (B) guessing.
   (C) how long it takes for an animal to perceive the echo.
   (D) how loud the call is that an animal emits.

12. Which best describes how the passage is organized?

   (A) A theory is explained and then proven wrong.
   (B) A concept is introduced and illustrations are provided.
   (C) An argument is introduced and then clarified.
   (D) Several terms are defined and explained.

CONTINUE TO THE NEXT PAGE

Questions 13-18

1   Residents of California are well acquainted with what it is like to live through an
2 earthquake. California is located along the San Andreas fault. Under the surface of the
3 earth are several tectonic plates. Where these plates meet up, and collide, there is great
4 potential for earthquakes as the two plates bump up against one another. When an
5 earthquakes occurs, the land above the colliding plates shakes violently, radiating out
6 from the epicenter. In California, the Pacific and North American plates meet, creating
7 the San Andreas fault along their boundaries. There are thousands of earthquakes along
8 this fault line every year, but most of them are so small that they cannot even be felt by
9 people. Every once in a while, however, there is a large earthquake in California.
10   Perhaps the most famous earthquake was the San Francisco earthquake of 1906.
11 On April 18, 1906, an earthquake struck Northern California that was so large that it
12 created a rupture that was 296 miles long. At that time, most of the land along this
13 rupture line was uninhabited. Unfortunately, the epicenter of the earthquake was below
14 the San Francisco Bay area. San Francisco was the ninth largest city in the United States
15 and its port was the center of trade and commerce for the entire west coast.
16   The earthquake itself did considerable damage to the city, but it was the fires that
17 came after the earthquake that left the city almost uninhabitable. Many homes and
18 businesses were heated and lit by natural gas and the earthquake ruptured the gas mains
19 that ran beneath the streets of the city. When these lines were ruptured, all it took was
20 a spark to start a fire. It is estimated that 80% of the damage to the city was caused by
21 the subsequent fires and not directly by the earthquake. While it is difficult to determine
22 the true number of casualties, it is estimated that over 3,000 people perished in the
23 earthquake of 1906 and the fires that followed.
24   In the aftermath of the earthquake, San Franciscans went about the harrowing task
25 of rebuilding. The damage was cleared and reconstruction began, this time with
26 stronger building codes to help prevent such a tragedy in the future.
27   On October 17, 1989, another strong earthquake struck in the San Francisco Bay
28 area. This time, there were many fewer casualties. Most of these casualties resulted
29 from the upper level of a freeway collapsing onto the lower level. Fortunately, traffic
30 was very light on this day because it was Game 3 of the World Series and the San
31 Francisco Giants were playing the Oakland Athletics, both teams based in the San
32 Francisco Bay area. When the ground started shaking at around 5 PM, there ordinarily
33 would have been many, many more cars on the freeway, but people were glued to the
34 baseball game rather than commuting. The live coverage of the game broadcast the
35 initial jolt of an earthquake for the first time in the United States.

CONTINUE TO THE NEXT PAGE

13. According to the passage, for what reason were casualties reduced in the 1989 San Francisco earthquake?

   (A) The 1989 earthquake was not as strong as the 1906 earthquake.
   (B) More people knew what to do during an earthquake.
   (C) Fewer people lived in San Francisco in 1989 than in 1906.
   (D) Many residents were watching the World Series during the 1989 earthquake.

14. It can be inferred from the passage that earthquakes in California

   (A) are more frequent than earthquakes in other places.
   (B) have not caused major damage.
   (C) have an unknown cause.
   (D) are predictable.

15. According to the passage, the greatest cause of casualties in the 1906 earthquake was

   (A) the lack of an evacuation plan.
   (B) underground gas mains that started fires.
   (C) residents who were trapped in buildings.
   (D) the large rupture that the earthquake caused.

16. In line 24, the word "harrowing" comes closest in meaning to

   (A) challenging.
   (B) delayed.
   (C) easy.
   (D) revised.

17. The main purpose of the first paragraph (lines 1-9) is to

   (A) introduce a character.
   (B) present an argument and its supports.
   (C) provide an explanation for an occurrence that will be discussed later.
   (D) explain why earthquakes are important.

18. How can the organization of the passage best be described?

   (A) A series of unrelated facts is described.
   (B) A thesis is presented and then disproved.
   (C) Different types of geological events are introduced.
   (D) An occurrence is explained and then illustrations are given.

CONTINUE TO THE NEXT PAGE

Questions 19-24

1   In the late 1960s and early 1970s, there were many psychology experiments being
2 conducted on university campuses across the United States. One of the most famous
3 studies was performed at Stanford University and came to be dubbed "the marshmallow
4 experiment".

5   In this study, several preschool-aged children were observed. An adult would offer
6 the child a treat, such as a marshmallow, that he or she could eat right away. The child
7 would also be given another option, though, if he or she was willing to delay eating the
8 marshmallow. If the child were able to not eat the treat in front of him or her for fifteen
9 minutes, then the child would receive a better treat, such as two marshmallows.

10   This experiment was meant to test a skill called "delayed gratification". Essentially,
11 delayed gratification means delaying one good outcome in order to achieve an even
12 better outcome. Some people view the ability to delay gratification as a measure of how
13 much self-control an individual has. A small number of children ate their marshmallow
14 as soon as the adult left the room. As time ticked by, though, more and more children
15 gave into temptation and only one-third of the children were able to wait the entire
16 fifteen minutes in order to receive the better treat.

17   The children employed many different strategies to avoid eating the marshmallows
18 in front of them. Some children would cover their eyes so that they could not see the
19 forbidden treat. Others acted out physically by kicking the desk or pulling on their hair.
20 Some other children played with the marshmallow as if it was a toy and not a tasty food.

21   Several years later, the researchers followed up with students who had participated
22 in the study as preschoolers. Ten years after the initial marshmallow experiment, the
23 students who were successful at delaying gratification as preschoolers were reported by
24 their parents to be more competent than other children their age. Even later, these same
25 students scored higher on academic tests.

CONTINUE TO THE NEXT PAGE

19. Which statement would the author most likely agree with?

    (A) People who can delay gratification are more likely to succeed.
    (B) It is hard to predict later behavior from preschool behavior.
    (C) Studies rarely provide usable results.
    (D) Preschoolers given marshmallows will succeed later.

20. In line 11, the word "outcome" comes closest in meaning to

    (A) exit.
    (B) result.
    (C) silence.
    (D) tour.

21. According to the passage, some students who did not eat the marshmallow used a strategy of

    (A) leaving the room.
    (B) pretending they didn't like marshmallows.
    (C) spitting on the marshmallow.
    (D) acting as if the marshmallow was not a desirable food.

22. What is the main point of the third paragraph (lines 10-16)?

    (A) It is very hard for children to resist temptation.
    (B) Marshmallows are very tasty.
    (C) Not eating marshmallows shows self-control.
    (D) Children do not make good study subjects.

23. As described in the passage, delayed gratification can be defined as

    (A) a skill to be learned.
    (B) the ability to defer what a person wants now for a later reward.
    (C) the key to success.
    (D) unrelated to self-control.

24. The passage provides evidence that supports which statement?

    (A) Self-control can be measured in an experiment.
    (B) There were few advances during the 1960s and 1970s.
    (C) The marshmallow experiment should not have been performed.
    (D) All of the strategies the children employed were effective.

CONTINUE TO THE NEXT PAGE

Questions 25-30

1   The world of art was changed forever when the Armory Show was staged in 1913.
2   The show was organized by the Association of American Painters and Sculptors and
3   held in a vast National Guard Armory located in New York City. The exhibition then
4   travelled to the Art Institute of Chicago and Boston's Copley Society of Art.
5   The Armory Show presented modern art to the American public for the first time
6   on a large scale. The Association of American Painters and Sculptors was formed in
7   1911 with the purpose of influencing American taste in art rather than following what
8   was already popular. Its founders had the vision of staging shows with works by artists
9   that had been rejected or ignored by other art venues. They wanted to exhibit artwork
10 that pushed the envelope and introduced Americans to the movement of modern art
11 that was blossoming in Europe.
12   Before the Armory Show, artwork exhibited in the United States tended to be
13 realistic in nature. American art enthusiasts were used to easily identifiable scenes from
14 life – a flower in first bloom, a group of picnickers on a lawn, a storm swept sea, and so
15 forth. In Europe there was a change brewing, however. Artists such as Henri Matisse
16 and Marcel Duchamp were advancing forms of painting that included abstractions, bold
17 exaggerations of shapes, and vivid colors rarely found in real life. The goal of the
18 Armory Show was to introduce this new modern art to an American audience.
19   Reaction to the exhibit in America was swift and not complimentary. Reviews
20 published in newspapers accused the artists and their supporters of insanity,
21 immorality, and anarchy. Former American president Theodore Roosevelt even
22 proclaimed, "that is not art."
23   During the exhibit, however, Paul Cézanne's *Hill of the Poor (View of the Domaine*
24 *Saint-Joseph)* was sold to the Metropolitan Museum of Art in New York City. This
25 marked the first time that a major art institution in the United States purchased a piece
26 of modern art. There were other successes as well. Jacques Villon sold all of his cubist
27 etchings and came to be supported by several New York art collectors that he met
28 through the Armory Show. One artwork that was widely ridiculed, Duchamp's *Nude*
29 *Descending a Staircase*, was sold at the Armory Show to a collector from San Francisco.
30 Modern art, which was considered so controversial at the Armory Show of 1913, has
31 since grown into a mainstay of the American art scene.

CONTINUE TO THE NEXT PAGE

25. The primary purpose of this passage is to explain

    (A) why Marcel Duchamp was ridiculed by Americans.
    (B) when the Association of American Painters and Sculptors was founded.
    (C) how the Armory Show changed American art.
    (D) the importance of art critics.

26. The passage implies that many Americans in 1913 were

    (A) bored with realistic paintings.
    (B) encouraging of new artists.
    (C) frequently travelling to Europe.
    (D) not open to new types of art.

27. It can be inferred from the passage that Jacques Villon was a

    (A) traditional painter.
    (B) newspaper critic.
    (C) modern artist.
    (D) collector.

28. According to the passage, the purpose of the Armory show was to

    (A) lead the United States into a new era of art.
    (B) help American artists continue a tradition.
    (C) provide a place for well-known artists to display their works.
    (D) limit European influence in American art.

29. Which best captures the main idea of the fourth paragraph (lines 19-22)?

    (A) Americans welcomed European artists.
    (B) Americans were generally not receptive to modern art at first.
    (C) The "new" art went largely unnoticed.
    (D) Many collectors were already buying modern art.

30. According to the passage, why was the sale of *Hill of the Poor (View of the Domaine Saint-Joseph)* a milestone?

    (A) The painting was previously lost.
    (B) The artist was not famous.
    (C) It was the first time a major American art institution bought a piece of modern art.
    (D) Theodore Roosevelt criticized the sale.

CONTINUE TO THE NEXT PAGE

Questions 31-36

1   Before the 19th century, it was widely accepted that illnesses and diseases were
2 caused by miasma, or a form of bad air. It was commonly believed that infections were
3 not passed from one person to another, but rather that the "bad air" caused multiple
4 people to develop a disease. Microorganisms had been observed after the invention of
5 the microscope in the 1600s. By the time that Louis Pasteur started performing
6 experiments in 1860, it was understood that these "worms" observed under the
7 microscope were the cause of disease but there was no explanation for where these
8 organisms developed from, or how they were transmitted. Many scientists believed in
9 spontaneous generation, or that the organisms could simply appear from the miasma.

10   Louis Pasteur set up vessels that contained a broth with nutrients that would
11 support the growth of bacteria. He then boiled these broths, effectively killing all living
12 organisms in these broths. The containers were then fitted with filters that would
13 prohibit small particles from entering the vessel. These containers with filters would
14 not grow any bacteria until the filter was removed and particles in the air were free to
15 infect the broth. This demonstrated that the bacteria did not spontaneously generate,
16 but rather that particles containing bacterial spores had to enter the broth in order for
17 the bacteria to grow.

18   Louis Pasteur had finally figured out how disease was transmitted from one person
19 to another. This important development allowed doctors to develop processes to reduce
20 disease transmission. Once it was understood that disease was passed from one person
21 from another by germs and not "bad air", then doctors knew what to target.

22   Louis Pasteur was able to apply his knowledge that boiling killed the bacteria in the
23 broths to save countless lives. Many people were made ill by organisms that grew in
24 milk, beer, and wine. Pasteur developed a process where these beverages could be
25 heated and then rapidly cooled, thereby reducing bacterial contamination and the
26 diseases that went along with it. The process was named pasteurization in his honor
27 and is now performed on almost all milk and juice sold in the United States. If liquids
28 were completely sterilized, or heated to the point that killed all living organisms, the
29 taste would be negatively affected. Louis Pasteur figured out that if a liquid was gently
30 heated and then cooled, enough of the bacteria would be killed that a person would not
31 be made sick, but the taste would not be drastically changed. This process not only
32 greatly reduced devastating diseases, such as cholera, but also allowed beverages to be
33 stored for a longer period of time without spoiling.

CONTINUE TO THE NEXT PAGE

31. The main purpose of this passage is to explain

    (A) what miasma is.
    (B) how germs are transmitted.
    (C) why milk spoils.
    (D) an important contribution of one scientist.

32. According to the passage, spontaneous generation

    (A) is important for understanding germs.
    (B) does not happen in reality.
    (C) explains disease transmission.
    (D) was proven to happen by Louis Pasteur.

33. According to the passage, the purpose of the filter in Pasteur's experiment was to

    (A) prevent air particles from entering the vessel.
    (B) completely seal off the broth from all air contact.
    (C) kill bacteria in the broth.
    (D) prevent sunlight from entering the vessel.

34. It can be inferred from the passage that

    (A) cholera was not an issue before pasteurization.
    (B) some bacteria contributes to a good taste.
    (C) sterilizing milk is the best solution to bacterial growth.
    (D) microscopes explained disease transmission.

35. Which word describes the author's attitude toward Louis Pasteur?

    (A) anxious
    (B) critical
    (C) nonchalant
    (D) respectful

36. How is this passage organized?

    (A) A theory is presented and then illustrations are provided.
    (B) A hypothesis is suggested and then proven to be correct in all situations.
    (C) Background information is provided, an experiment is described, and the importance of the results is explained.
    (D) Competing theories are debated, then all but one are proven wrong.

STOP

IF YOU HAVE TIME LEFT YOU MAY CHECK YOUR ANSWERS IN THIS SECTION ONLY

Mathematics Achievement

47 questions

40 minutes

Each math question has four answer choices after it. Choose the answer choice that best answers the question.

Make sure that you fill in the correct answer on your answer sheet. You may write in the test booklet.

SAMPLE QUESTION:

1. Which number can be divided by 4 with nothing left over?

    (A) 6
    ● 12
    (C) 15
    (D) 22

Since 12 can be divided by 4 with no remainder, circle B is filled in.

STOP

DO NOT MOVE ON TO THE SECTION UNTIL TOLD TO

1. What is the least common multiple of 10, 12, and 16?

    (A) 2
    (B) 4
    (C) 240
    (D) 1,920

2. The sum of 8,692 + 6,429 is equal to

    (A) 15,121
    (B) 15,131
    (C) 15,221
    (D) 15,231

3. The expression 6.4 + 0.37 + 42 is equal to

    (A) 47.95
    (B) 48.77
    (C) 48.96
    (D) 49.37

4. The larger rectangle below is divided into equal sections.

    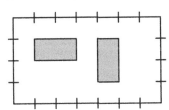

    What fraction of the larger rectangle is shaded?

    (A) $\dfrac{1}{28}$

    (B) $\dfrac{1}{16}$

    (C) $\dfrac{1}{8}$

    (D) $\dfrac{1}{7}$

CONTINUE TO THE NEXT PAGE

5. The average of a group of numbers is 12, the range of these numbers is 7, and the mode of these numbers is 15. Which of the following could be the median of these numbers?

    (A) 7
    (B) 8
    (C) 13
    (D) 17

6. The number of cupcakes at the bake sale this year increased by 200% compared to the number of cupcakes at last year's bake sale. The number of cupcakes this year was how many times the number of cupcakes last year?

    (A) 2
    (B) 3
    (C) 3.5
    (D) 4

7. If $4■ = 3Δ$ and one $Δ$ is 20, then what is $■$ equal to?

    (A) 15
    (B) 18
    (C) 24
    (D) 60

8. Which number has only itself and 1 as positive factors?

    (A) 4
    (B) 9
    (C) 39
    (D) 41

9. If $3n + 4 = 13$, then what is the value of $6n + 8$?

    (A) 3
    (B) 26
    (C) 30
    (D) 39

CONTINUE TO THE NEXT PAGE

10. A bookstore sells books at 20% off of the list price. During a clearance sale, the store took an additional 20% off of the already discounted price. If the list price of a book was $14, then what is its clearance price?

    (A) $8.40
    (B) $8.96
    (C) $9.50
    (D) $11.20

11. If $\dfrac{t}{3} = \dfrac{t+4}{-3}$, then what is the value of t?

    (A) -2
    (B) -1
    (C) 2
    (D) 4

12. A taxi cab driver charges $3 for the first mile and $1.20 for each additional mile. Which equation would allow a passenger to figure out the total cost (C) of a ride that is M miles long?

    (A) $C = 3M + 1.2M$
    (B) $C = 3M + 1.2$
    (C) $C = 3 + 1.2M$
    (D) $C = 3 + 1.2(M - 1)$

13. What is the value of the expression $3 + 4 \times 7 - 5$?

    (A) 14
    (B) 20
    (C) 26
    (D) 44

14. Jacqueline earns $96 a week at her afterschool job. She saves $\dfrac{1}{6}$ of that money each week. After 3 weeks, how much money will she have saved?

    (A) $16
    (B) $32
    (C) $48
    (D) $56

CONTINUE TO THE NEXT PAGE

15. Mr. Hampton's class grew six types of grasses for three weeks. At the end of three weeks, they measured the highest height for each type of grass. Their results are shown below.

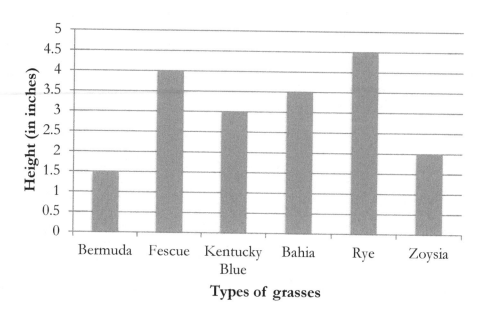

What was the difference between the greatest height and the least height of the grasses measured?

(A) 3 inches

(B) 4 inches

(C) 4.5 inches

(D) 6 inches

16. In the figure below, the distance from A to B is 4 and the distance from C to D is 3.

If the distance from A to D is 12, then what is the distance from B to C?

(A) 4

(B) 5

(C) 6

(D) 7

CONTINUE TO THE NEXT PAGE

17. In the figure below triangle *DEF* is similar to triangle *ABC*.

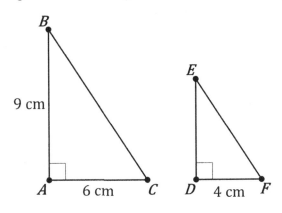

What is the area of triangle *DEF*?

(area of a triangle $= \frac{1}{2} \times b \times h$)

(A)   3 cm²

(B)   4 cm²

(C)   6 cm²

(D)   12 cm²

18. Use the figure below.

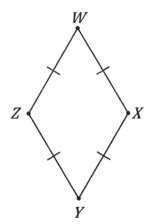

Which word best describes quadrilateral *WXYZ*?

(A)   rhombus

(B)   trapezoid

(C)   square

(D)   rectangle

CONTINUE TO THE NEXT PAGE

19. Norm has packed in his suitcase a white shirt, a yellow shirt, and a green shirt. He has also packed four solid-colored pairs of pants that are white, tan, green, and orange. Norm wants to figure out the probability that he will randomly select a shirt and a pair of pants that are the same color. Which table is correctly shaded to help Norm figure out the answer?

(A)

white shirt – white pants *(shaded)*	white shirt – tan pants	white shirt – green pants *(shaded)*	white shirt – orange pants
yellow shirt – white pants *(shaded)*	yellow shirt – tan pants	yellow shirt – green pants *(shaded)*	yellow shirt – orange pants
green shirt – white pants	green shirt – tan pants	green shirt – green pants	green shirt – orange pants

(B)

white shirt – white pants	white shirt – tan pants	white shirt – green pants	white shirt – orange pants *(shaded)*
yellow shirt – white pants *(shaded)*	yellow shirt – tan pants *(shaded)*	yellow shirt – green pants	yellow shirt – orange pants
green shirt – white pants	green shirt – tan pants	green shirt – green pants *(shaded)*	green shirt – orange pants

(C)

white shirt – white pants *(shaded)*	white shirt – tan pants	white shirt – green pants	white shirt – orange pants
yellow shirt – white pants	yellow shirt – tan pants	yellow shirt – green pants	yellow shirt – orange pants
green shirt – white pants	green shirt – tan pants	green shirt – green pants *(shaded)*	green shirt – orange pants

(D)

white shirt – white pants *(shaded)*	white shirt – tan pants	white shirt – green pants	white shirt – orange pants
yellow shirt – white pants	yellow shirt – tan pants	yellow shirt – green pants	yellow shirt – orange pants *(shaded)*
green shirt – white pants	green shirt – tan pants	green shirt – green pants *(shaded)*	green shirt – orange pants

CONTINUE TO THE NEXT PAGE

20. What is the slope of the line $2x + 7y = 5$?

(A) $-\dfrac{7}{2}$

(B) $-\dfrac{2}{7}$

(C) $\dfrac{2}{7}$

(D) $\dfrac{7}{2}$

21. Rectangle *GHIJ* and rectangle *KLMN* are similar to one another.

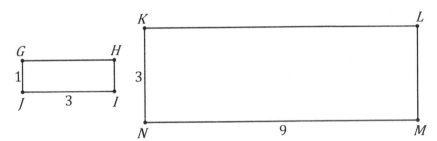

What is the ratio of the area of rectangle *GHIJ* to the area of rectangle *KLMN*?

(A) 1 to 3

(B) 1 to 9

(C) 3 to 1

(D) 9 to 1

22. Which answer choice shows a network with routes from *G* to *K*, *J* to *H*, *H* to *L*, and *K* to *I*, and includes NO other routes?

(A)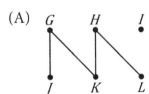

(B)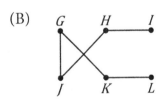

(C)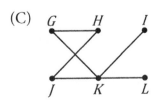

(D)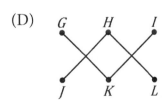

CONTINUE TO THE NEXT PAGE

23. Use the circle below.

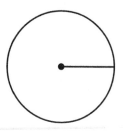

Note: Area of a circle $= \pi r^2$

What is the radius, r, of the circle shown if its area is 9π?

(A) 3
(B) 4.5
(C) 6
(D) 9

24. Troy surveyed his friends asking them how many cousins they had. His results are shown below in the stem and leaf plot below.

0	2 2 3 5 7 9 9
1	0 0 1 4 6
2	1 1 3
3	0 0 1 2 4

2 | 1   represents 21 cousins

How many friends did Troy survey?

(A) 16
(B) 19
(C) 20
(D) 24

CONTINUE TO THE NEXT PAGE

25. Santos answered 24 out of 30 questions correctly on a quiz. What percent of the questions did he answer correctly?

    (A) 60%
    (B) 80%
    (C) 85%
    (D) 90%

26. A box of crayons has 5 red crayons, 6 yellow crayons, 3 green crayons, and 4 blue crayons. If a crayon is randomly picked, what is the probability that crayon will be yellow?

    (A) $\frac{1}{6}$

    (B) $\frac{1}{3}$

    (C) $\frac{1}{2}$

    (D) $\frac{2}{3}$

27. If $m - 4 + 6 = n$, then what is the value of $m - n$?

    (A) -2
    (B) -1
    (C) 0
    (D) 2

CONTINUE TO THE NEXT PAGE

28. On the number line below, Point *B* (not shown) represents a number that is 15 greater than the number represented by Point *A*.

What number does Point B represent?

(A) −20
(B) −5
(C) 5
(D) 10

29. Jessica surveyed 200 people, asking them their favorite type of movie. Her results are shown in the circle graph below.

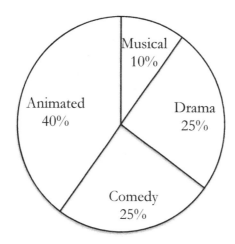

How many people told Jessica that their favorite kind of movie was animated movies?

(A) 40
(B) 50
(C) 80
(D) 100

CONTINUE TO THE NEXT PAGE

30. The rectangle below has a perimeter of 50 cm.

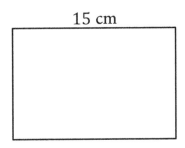

15 cm

What is the width of the rectangle?

(A)   4 cm
(B)   5 cm
(C)   10 cm
(D)   17.5 cm

31. Of the $\frac{2}{3}$ of a class that said they like chocolate ice cream, 90% said they also like vanilla ice cream. What percent of the class said they like both chocolate and vanilla ice cream?

(A)   45%
(B)   60%
(C)   66.7%
(D)   70%

32. If $\frac{5}{6}$ of a bucket is filled in one minute, how many seconds would it take to fill the rest of the bucket if it is filled at the same rate?

(A)   12
(B)   17.5
(C)   20
(D)   25

CONTINUE TO THE NEXT PAGE

33. Use the chart below to answer the question.

$$2^1 = 2$$
$$2^2 = 4$$
$$2^3 = 8$$
$$2^4 = 16$$
$$2^5 = 32$$
$$2^6 = 64$$

According to this pattern, what will be the last digit of 2^9?

(A) 2
(B) 4
(C) 8
(D) 6

34. The value of 6.92×0.04 is approximately

(A) 0.028
(B) 0.28
(C) 2.8
(D) 28

35. If the volume of a cube is 64 cm^3, then what is its surface area?

(A) 16 cm^2
(B) 32 cm^2
(C) 64 cm^2
(D) 96 cm^2

CONTINUE TO THE NEXT PAGE

36. Alyssa is plotting a trapezoid as shown below.

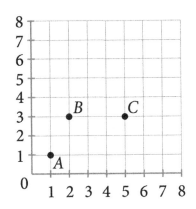

Alyssa plotted three of the vertices of the trapezoid, labeled as points A, B, and C. What are the coordinates of the fourth vertex that she still needs to plot?

(A) $(0, 3)$
(B) $(1, 6)$
(C) $(6, 1)$
(D) $(7, 2)$

37. Which expression is equivalent to $\dfrac{8(\sqrt{36} + 4x)}{\sqrt{16}}$?

(A) $12 + 8x$
(B) $12 + 4x$
(C) $\dfrac{4(\sqrt{36} + 4x)}{4}$
(D) $\dfrac{8(10x)}{4}$

CONTINUE TO THE NEXT PAGE

38. Use the division problem below to answer the question.

$$
\begin{array}{r}
26 \\
11{\overline{\smash{\big)}\,2\blacksquare6}} \\
\underline{22} \\
66 \\
\underline{66}
\end{array}
$$

What digit does the ■ represent in the above division problem?

(A) 2

(B) 6

(C) 8

(D) 9

39. Line q is perpendicular to line m. If the equation of line m is $y = \dfrac{2}{3}x - 3\dfrac{2}{3}$ and the two lines intersect at the point $(4, -1)$, then what is the equation of line q?

(A) $y = -\dfrac{3}{2}x - 5$

(B) $y = -\dfrac{3}{2}x + 5$

(C) $y = \dfrac{3}{2}x - 5$

(D) $y = \dfrac{3}{2}x + 5$

40. Ricky wants to raise $300 for a school trip by selling candy bars. He can buy a box of 80 chocolate bars for $45. If he wants to sell about 150 candy bars, how much must he charge for each candy bar in order to make a $300 profit? Profit is equal to revenue minus cost.

(A) $1.50

(B) $2.00

(C) $2.60

(D) $3.00

CONTINUE TO THE NEXT PAGE

41. Which equation is equivalent to $b = \dfrac{c}{3} + 4$?

    (A) $3b - c = 4$

    (B) $3(b - c) = 4$

    (C) $c + 4 = \dfrac{b}{3}$

    (D) $\dfrac{1}{3}c = b - 4$

42. If Carolyn runs 24 miles every four weeks, then how many miles would she run in six weeks at that rate?

    (A) 36 miles

    (B) 42 miles

    (C) 48 miles

    (D) 144 miles

43. Which graph shows the solution for $x - 5 > -3$?

    (A)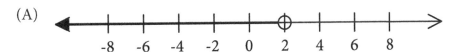

    (B)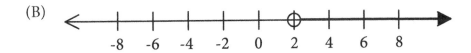

    (C)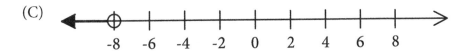

    (D)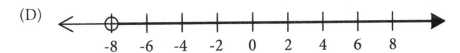

CONTINUE TO THE NEXT PAGE

44. The expression $5(W + 7)$ is equivalent to

    (A) $W + 35$
    (B) $5W + 7$
    (C) $5W + 35$
    (D) $7(W + 5)$

45. Which is equivalent to 1.4 hours?

    (A) 1 hour 4 minutes

    (B) 1 hour 16 minutes

    (C) 1 hour 24 minutes

    (D) 1 hour 30 minutes

46. Triangle *GHI* was transformed in order to create triangle *G'H'I'*.

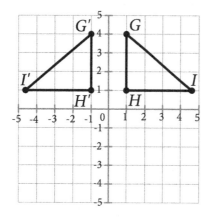

    Which transformation was performed?

    (A) a reflection
    (B) a slide
    (C) a turn
    (D) a rotation

CONTINUE TO THE NEXT PAGE

47. Jesse took a survey asking students what their favorite subject is. The results are shown in the circle graph below.

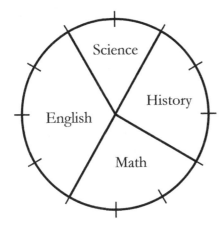

What percent of students said that history was their favorite subject?

(A) 20%
(B) 25%
(C) 30%
(D) 45%

STOP

IF YOU HAVE TIME LEFT YOU MAY CHECK YOUR ANSWERS IN THIS SECTION ONLY

Essay

You will be given 30 minutes to plan and write an essay. The topic is printed on the next page. *Make sure that you write about this topic. Do NOT choose another topic.*

This essay gives you the chance to show your thinking and how well you can express your ideas. Do not worry about filling all of the space provided. The quality is more important than how much you write. You should write more than a brief paragraph, though.

A copy of this essay will be sent to the schools that you apply to. Make sure that you only write in the appropriate area on the answer sheet. Please print so that the admissions officers can understand what you wrote.

On the next page is the topic sheet. There is room on this sheet to make notes and collect your thoughts. The final essay should be written on the two lined sheets provided in the answer sheet, however. Make sure that you copy your topic at the top of the first lined page. Write only in blue or black ink. (Answer sheets are found at the beginning of this book and you can go to www.testprepworks.com/student/download to download additional copies.)

REMINDER: Please remember to write the topic on the top of the first lined page in your answer sheet.

> What is the most important part of the school day?
>
> Why is it the most important part of the school day?

- Write only about this topic
- Only the lined sheets will be sent to schools
- Use only blue or black ink

Notes

_____

_____

_____

_____

_____

_____

_____

_____

_____

_____

_____

_____

_____

_____

_____

_____

_____

_____

_____

Answers

Verbal Reasoning Answers

Correct answer	Your answer	Put a checkmark here if you answered the question correctly
1. C		
2. B		
3. A		
4. D		
5. B		
6. C		
7. A		
8. C		
9. D		
10. D		
11. B		
12. C		
13. D		
14. A		
15. B		
16. C		
17. A		
18. A		
19. C		
20. B		
21. D		
22. C		

23. A		
24. A		
25. B		
26. D		
27. C		
28. C		
29. A		
30. D		
31. B		
32. C		
33. A		
34. C		
35. D		
36. B		
37. A		
38. C		
39. D		
40. B		
Total questions answered correctly: _____		

Interpreting Your Verbal Reasoning Score

On the ISEE, your raw score is the number of questions that you answered correctly on each section. Nothing is subtracted for the questions that you answered incorrectly.

Your raw score is then converted into a scaled score. This scaled score is then converted into a percentile score. Remember that it is the percentile score that schools are looking at. Your percentile score compares you just to other students in your grade.

Below is a chart that gives a very rough conversion between your raw score on the practice Verbal Reasoning section and a percentile score.

PLEASE NOTE – The purpose of this chart is to let you see how the scoring works, not to give you an accurate percentile score. You will need to complete the official practice test in *What to Expect on the ISEE*, available for download from ERB at www.erblearn.org, in order to get a more accurate percentile score.

Middle Level Verbal Reasoning

Applicants to Grade 7			
Percentile score	25th	50th	75th
Approximate raw score needed	19-20	25-26	29-30

Applicants to Grade 8			
Percentile score	25th	50th	75th
Approximate raw score needed	24-25	28-29	32-33

Quantitative Reasoning Answers

Correct answer	Your answer	Put a checkmark here if you answered the question correctly
1. C		
2. B		
3. D		
4. A		
5. B		
6. C		
7. A		
8. D		
9. D		
10. A		
11. B		
12. B		
13. C		
14. A		
15. D		
16. B		
17. C		
18. A		
19. B		
20. B		
21. B		
22. A		
23. C		
24. A		

25. A		
26. C		
27. D		
28. C		
29. B		
30. B		
31. A		
32. B		
33. A		
34. C		
35. D		
36. A		
37. D		
Total questions answered correctly: _____		

Interpreting Your Quantitative Reasoning Score

On the ISEE, your raw score is the number of questions that you answered correctly on each section. Nothing is subtracted for the questions that you answered incorrectly.

Your raw score is then converted into a scaled score. This scaled score is then converted into a percentile score. Remember that it is the percentile score that schools are looking at. Your percentile score compares you just to other students in your grade.

Below is a chart that gives a very rough conversion between your raw score on the practice Quantitative Reasoning section and a percentile score.

PLEASE NOTE – The purpose of this chart is to let you see how the scoring works, not to give you an accurate percentile score. You will need to complete the official practice test in *What to Expect on the ISEE*, available for download from ERB at www.erblearn.org, in order to get a more accurate percentile score.

Middle Level Quantitative Reasoning

Applicants to Grade 7			
Percentile score	25th	50th	75th
Approximate raw score needed	16-17	20-21	24-25

Applicants to Grade 8			
Percentile score	25th	50th	75th
Approximate raw score needed	20-21	23-24	26-27

Reading Comprehension Answers

Correct answer	Your answer	Put a checkmark here if you answered the question correctly
1. C		
2. B		
3. A		
4. D		
5. B		
6. A		
7. D		
8. C		
9. A		
10. B		
11. C		
12. B		
13. D		
14. A		
15. B		
16. A		
17. C		
18. D		
19. A		
20. B		
21. D		
22. A		
23. B		
24. A		

25. C		
26. D		
27. C		
28. A		
29. B		
30. C		
31. D		
32. B		
33. A		
34. B		
35. D		
36. C		
Total questions answered correctly: _____		

Interpreting Your Reading Comprehension Score

On the ISEE, your raw score is the number of questions that you answered correctly on each section. Nothing is subtracted for the questions that you answered incorrectly.

Your raw score is then converted into a scaled score. This scaled score is then converted into a percentile score. Remember that it is the percentile score that schools are looking at. Your percentile score compares you just to other students in your grade.

Below is a chart that gives a very rough conversion between your raw score on the practice Reading Comprehension section and a percentile score.

PLEASE NOTE – The purpose of this chart is to let you see how the scoring works, not to give you an accurate percentile score. You will need to complete the official practice test in *What to Expect on the ISEE*, available for download from ERB at www.erblearn.org, in order to get a more accurate percentile score.

Middle Level Reading Comprehension

Applicants to Grade 7			
Percentile score	25th	50th	75th
Approximate raw score needed	11-12	17-18	22-23

Applicants to Grade 8			
Percentile score	25th	50th	75th
Approximate raw score needed	16-17	21-22	25-26

Mathematics Achievement Answers

Correct answer	Your answer	Put a checkmark here if you answered the question correctly
1. C		
2. A		
3. B		
4. D		
5. C		
6. B		
7. A		
8. D		
9. B		
10. B		
11. A		
12. D		
13. C		
14. C		
15. A		
16. B		
17. D		
18. A		
19. C		
20. B		
21. B		
22. D		
23. A		
24. C		

25. B		
26. B		
27. A		
28. D		
29. C		
30. C		
31. B		
32. A		
33. A		
34. B		
35. D		
36. C		
37. A		
38. C		
39. B		
40. C		
41. D		
42. A		
43. B		
44. C		
45. C		
46. A		
47. B		
Total questions answered correctly: _____		

Interpreting Your Mathematics Achievement Score

On the ISEE, your raw score is the number of questions that you answered correctly on each section. Nothing is subtracted for the questions that you answered incorrectly.

Your raw score is then converted into a scaled score. This scaled score is then converted into a percentile score. Remember that it is the percentile score that schools are looking at. Your percentile score compares you just to other students in your grade.

Below is a chart that gives a very rough conversion between your raw score on the practice Mathematics Achievement section and a percentile score.

PLEASE NOTE – The purpose of this chart is to let you see how the scoring works, not to give you an accurate percentile score. You will need to complete the official practice test in *What to Expect on the ISEE*, available for download from ERB at www.erblearn.org, in order to get a more accurate percentile score.

Middle Level Mathematics Achievement

Applicants to Grade 7			
Percentile score	25th	50th	75th
Approximate raw score needed	32-33	37-38	42-43

Applicants to Grade 8			
Percentile score	25th	50th	75th
Approximate raw score needed	35-36	39-40	43-44

Practice Test 2

Verbal Reasoning

40 questions

20 minutes

The Verbal Reasoning section has two parts. When you finish Part One, be sure to keep working on Part Two. For each answer that you choose, make sure to fill in the corresponding circle on the answer sheet.

Part One – Synonyms

The questions in Part One each have a word in all capital letters with four answer choices after it. Choose the answer choice with the word that comes closest in meaning to the word in all capital letters.

SAMPLE QUESTION:

1. SPEEDY:

   (A) loud
   (B) messy
   ● quick
   (D) small

Part Two – Sentence Completions

The questions in Part Two each have a sentence with one blank. The blank takes the place of a word that is missing. The sentence has four answer choices after it. Choose the answer choice that would best complete the meaning of the sentence.

SAMPLE QUESTION:

1. Since the weather is getting warmer every day, it is particularly important to -------- more water.

   (A) create
   ● drink
   (C) leave
   (D) waste

STOP

DO NOT MOVE ON TO THE SECTION UNTIL TOLD TO

Part One – Synonyms

Directions: Choose the word that is closest in meaning to the word that is in all capital letters.

1. GUARANTEE:

   (A) abate
   (B) focus
   (C) promise
   (D) structure

2. ROUTINE:

   (A) amiable
   (B) honorable
   (C) outcast
   (D) regular

3. STUN:

   (A) dissolve
   (B) shock
   (C) tempt
   (D) weep

4. CONDEMN:

   (A) blame
   (B) liberate
   (C) need
   (D) provoke

5. CORDIAL:

   (A) blunt
   (B) friendly
   (C) hostile
   (D) mutual

6. RECKLESS:

   (A) busy
   (B) consistent
   (C) irresponsible
   (D) nimble

7. CHERISH:

   (A) discard
   (B) index
   (C) signify
   (D) treasure

8. DISMANTLE:

   (A) criticize
   (B) perform
   (C) sponsor
   (D) wreck

9. CAMOUFLAGE:

   (A) disguise
   (B) flourish
   (C) jiggle
   (D) withhold

10. MASSIVE:

   (A) contaminated
   (B) enormous
   (C) hardy
   (D) tedious

CONTINUE TO THE NEXT PAGE

11. AUTHENTIC:

    (A) chronic
    (B) definite
    (C) genuine
    (D) wayward

12. EVADE:

    (A) avoid
    (B) capsize
    (C) gamble
    (D) recall

13. ORNATE:

    (A) deliberate
    (B) fancy
    (C) musical
    (D) purified

14. CLARIFY:

    (A) begrudge
    (B) divert
    (C) explain
    (D) hobble

15. ADJACENT:

    (A) bordering
    (B) disorganized
    (C) precise
    (D) stolen

16. CONSCIOUS:

    (A) aware
    (B) familiar
    (C) precious
    (D) slender

17. CULTIVATE:

    (A) baste
    (B) defend
    (C) grow
    (D) ship

18. ARDENT:

    (A) concealed
    (B) passionate
    (C) sorrowful
    (D) tame

19. IRK:

    (A) annoy
    (B) favor
    (C) illustrate
    (D) treat

20. CURTAIL:

    (A) acknowledge
    (B) chat
    (C) limit
    (D) puncture

21. ROBUST:

    (A) ambitious
    (B) neat
    (C) proper
    (D) strong

CONTINUE TO THE NEXT PAGE

Part Two – Sentence completions

Directions: Choose the word to best complete the sentence.

22. The Ford Model T, the first affordable car in America, became a(n) ---------- success when it was introduced and sales quickly skyrocketed.

    (A) academic
    (B) imperfect
    (C) singular
    (D) tidy

23. In order to avoid predators, voles will ------- into a pile of leaves so that they are almost invisible.

    (A) eat
    (B) nestle
    (C) originate
    (D) twinge

24. The poet and politician Dante was ------- from his home in Florence and was never allowed to return.

    (A) banished
    (B) encouraged
    (C) governed
    (D) thrilled

25. Union Station in Washington, D.C., was in -------- condition and the ceiling almost collapsed before renovations began.

    (A) appealing
    (B) dire
    (C) jovial
    (D) valiant

CONTINUE TO THE NEXT PAGE

26. While it would seem that polar plunges, where swimmers jump into freezing cold water, would be very unpleasant, many participants actually claim that the experience is ---------.

   (A) abundant
   (B) corrupt
   (C) hazardous
   (D) invigorating

27. It is undesirable for a bathroom window to be ----------, rather an opaque glass is often used instead.

   (A) familiar
   (B) mundane
   (C) transparent
   (D) whimsical

28. Pax Romana was a time period known for peace because there was a ------- in the aggressive expansion of the Roman Empire and therefore fewer wars.

   (A) growth
   (B) lull
   (C) memory
   (D) spike

29. Unfortunately, the poems of Emily Dickinson were heavily -------- by editors who thought that her writing style was not suitable for publication as the poems were written.

   (A) enhanced
   (B) justified
   (C) modified
   (D) read

30. The clay soldiers of China are surprisingly lifelike for --------- objects.

   (A) inanimate
   (B) jaded
   (C) mortal
   (D) reasonable

CONTINUE TO THE NEXT PAGE

31. Foxes are often described as being ------- because of the stealthy and quiet way that they often move.

   (A) anxious
   (B) domestic
   (C) prone
   (D) sly

32. Between 1935 and 1945 jazz music was at the height of its popularity, but since then attendance at jazz concerts has -------

   (A) ebbed
   (B) grown
   (C) overwhelmed
   (D) specified

33. When plastic was first introduced at the World's Fair in 1862 it was hailed as a miracle material since it was --------- and could be shaped into any form.

   (A) flawed
   (B) pliable
   (C) suitable
   (D) transported

34. During the American Civil War, George Barnard was one of the first photographers to create -------- by piecing together several photographs in order to give a wide view of landscapes.

   (A) cores
   (B) disbelief
   (C) panoramas
   (D) tracks

35. Cynthia was surprised when she did not receive a newspaper on Sunday, but when she called the newspaper company they told her that her subscription had -------.

   (A) begrudged
   (B) dwelled
   (C) embraced
   (D) lapsed

CONTINUE TO THE NEXT PAGE

36. Although palm trees are known for growing in warm climates, Blue Palms are surprisingly -------- in colder temperatures.

    (A) crafty
    (B) genuine
    (C) hardy
    (D) vulnerable

37. Albert Einstein's ---------- method of thinking led to breakthroughs in physics that no one had imagined possible.

    (A) casual
    (B) devout
    (C) mundane
    (D) unconventional

38. It can be very difficult to judge whether another person's actions are accidental or are ----------.

    (A) deliberate
    (B) identical
    (C) lavish
    (D) unintended

39. The aloe vera plant has healing properties so it is often used to -------- pain when a person gets a bad sunburn.

    (A) alleviate
    (B) fabricate
    (C) portray
    (D) salvage

40. A rhinoceros' horn is used only for protection and not for hunting prey since a rhinoceros is a -------.

    (A) carnivore
    (B) herbivore
    (C) mammal
    (D) predator

STOP

IF YOU HAVE TIME LEFT YOU MAY CHECK YOUR ANSWERS IN THIS SECTION ONLY

Quantitative Reasoning

37 questions

35 minutes

Each math question has four answer choices after it. Choose the answer choice that best answers the question.

Make sure that you fill in the correct answer on your answer sheet. You may write in the test booklet.

SAMPLE QUESTION:

1. What is the perimeter of a rectangle that has a length of 3 cm and a width of 5 cm?

    $(P = 2l + 2w)$

    (A) 6 cm
    (B) 10 cm
    (C) 8 cm
    (●) 16 cm

The correct answer is 16 cm and circle D is filled in.

STOP

DO NOT MOVE ON TO THE SECTION UNTIL TOLD TO

Part One – Word Problems

1. A tank that is $\frac{1}{4}$ full currently contains 150 gallons of water. How many gallons of water would this tank hold when it is full?

    (A) 150
    (B) 300
    (C) 450
    (D) 600

2. In Mr. Schwartz's class, 12 students took a test. The histogram below shows the range of scores that the students received.

    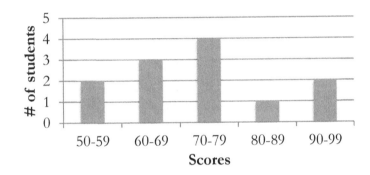

    Which of the following measures could never equal one of the student scores that were used to make the histogram?

    (A) median
    (B) range
    (C) mode
    (D) mean

CONTINUE TO THE NEXT PAGE

3. The figure below shows a pattern that could be folded into a three dimensional shape.

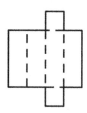

When folded, the pattern would create which polyhedron?

(A)

(B)

(C)

(D)

4. A furniture store gives bonus points according to the number of items purchased, as shown in the table below.

Number of items purchased	Bonus points awarded
1	3
2	9
3	27

If a customer received 243 bonus points, how many items did he purchase?

(A) 4
(B) 5
(C) 27
(D) 81

CONTINUE TO THE NEXT PAGE

5. The shape below was built using smaller cubes.

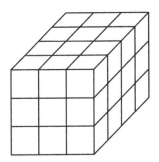

How many smaller cubes were used?

(A) 9
(B) 27
(C) 36
(D) 64

6. The graph below shows the distance from the school versus time for four different cars.

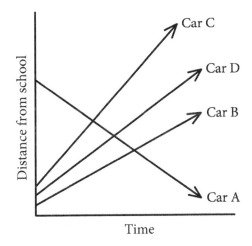

Which car is driving away from the school at the greatest speed?

(A) A
(B) B
(C) C
(D) D

CONTINUE TO THE NEXT PAGE

7. Which of the following numbers is closest to 2?

   (A) 2.2
   (B) 2.15
   (C) 2.02
   (D) 1.99

8. Use the picture below to answer the question.

   Which answer choice shows the above picture rotated 180 degrees?

   (A)

   (B)

   (C)

   (D)

9. If 5 hols = 1 biks then 5 hols + 4 biks is equal to how many hols?

   (A) 9
   (B) 18
   (C) 24
   (D) 25

10. Ross has been watching a movie for 32 minutes and is $\frac{2}{5}$ of the way through the movie. How long is the entire movie, in minutes?

   (A) 64
   (B) 72
   (C) 80
   (D) 160

CONTINUE TO THE NEXT PAGE

11. Christy is using a random number generator in order to pick numbers. When Christy pushes a button, the machine prints out a number from 1 to 9. If Christy pushes the button twice, what is the probability that both numbers printed out will be less than 5?

(A) $\dfrac{4}{81}$

(B) $\dfrac{16}{81}$

(C) $\dfrac{2}{9}$

(D) $\dfrac{4}{9}$

12. The two cubes below have volumes (*V*) that are proportional.

Figure 1   **Figure 2**

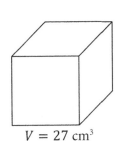   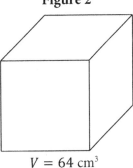

$V = 27$ cm^3 $V = 64$ cm^3

What is the ratio of the surface area of the cube in Figure 1 to the surface area of the cube in Figure 2?

(A) 3 to 4

(B) 4 to 3

(C) 9 to 16

(D) 16 to 9

13. The square root of 120 is closest to which number?

(A) 11

(B) 12

(C) 13

(D) 15

CONTINUE TO THE NEXT PAGE

14. In the pattern below, there are 9 square tiles each with an area of 1 ft².

If this pattern is repeated 24 times in order to cover a wall, then the portion of that wall covered in shaded tile will be

(A) 4 ft²
(B) 5 ft²
(C) 72 ft²
(D) 112 ft²

15. The mean is 12 for a group of 6 numbers. What number must be added to this set if the mean of this new set is to be 4 less than the original set?

(A) −18
(B) −16
(C) −12
(D) −4

16. Brendan had a handful of dimes. He traded in his dimes for an equal number of quarters. The value of his quarters is $1.35 greater than the value of his dimes was. How many quarters does Brendan have now?

(A) 9
(B) 10
(C) 11
(D) 12

17. If p and q are whole numbers and the product of p and q is 20, then what is the greatest possible value for $p + q$?

(A) 9
(B) 11
(C) 21
(D) 24

CONTINUE TO THE NEXT PAGE

18. At the start of the day, there were 46 coins in a fountain. By the end of the day, the number of coins in the fountain had increased by 200%. How many coins were in the fountain at the end of the day?

    (A) 23
    (B) 92
    (C) 115
    (D) 138

19. On Sunday, Ann sent flowers to 2 friends. On Monday, those two people each sent flowers to two of their friends, who on Tuesday then sent flowers to two of their friends. This pattern repeated until Friday. Which expression would help Ann figure out how many total people had received flowers?

    (A) $1 + 2^5$
    (B) $1 + 2^6$
    (C) $1 + 2 + 2^2 + 2^3 + 2^4 + 2^5$
    (D) $2 + 2^2 + 2^3 + 2^4 + 2^5 + 2^6$

20. If $m + 3$ is 4 more than r, then $m + 12$ is how many more than r?

    (A) 13
    (B) 15
    (C) 19
    (D) 21

CONTINUE TO THE NEXT PAGE

Part Two – Quantitative Comparisons

Directions: Use the information in the question to compare the quantities in Columns A and B. After comparing the two quantities, choose the correct answer choice:

(A) Quantity in Column A is greater.

(B) Quantity in Column B is greater.

(C) The quantities in Column A and Column B are equal.

(D) Cannot be determined from the information given.

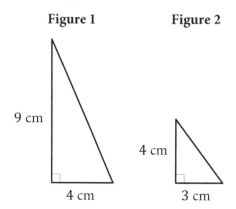

Figure 1   **Figure 2**

9 cm

4 cm

4 cm   3 cm

<u>**Column A**</u>   <u>**Column B**</u>

21.   Area of a triangle similar to Figure 1   Area of a triangle similar to Figure 2

with a scale factor of $\dfrac{3}{4}$ with a scale factor of $\dfrac{4}{3}$

CONTINUE TO THE NEXT PAGE

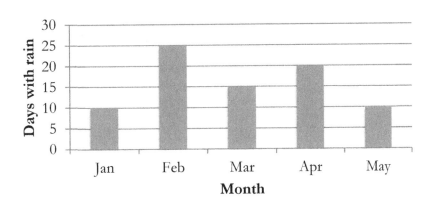

	Column A	Column B
22.	Median number of days of rain per month	Mean number of days of rain per month

	Column A	Column B
23.	The number of multiples of 7 between 2 and 48	The number of multiples of 7 between 6 and 43

	Column A	Column B
24.	$\sqrt{4 + 25}$	$\sqrt{4} + \sqrt{25}$

The price of an $80 shirt is reduced by 20% for a sale. This new price is then reduced by 10% for clearance.

	Column A	Column B
25.	The clearance price of the shirt	$56

CONTINUE TO THE NEXT PAGE

Column A	Column B
26. x	$\dfrac{1}{x}$

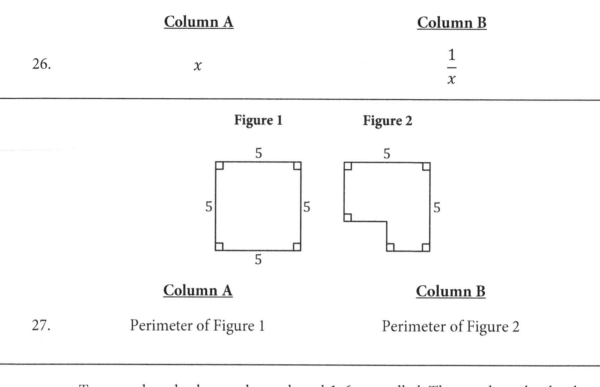

Column A	Column B
27. Perimeter of Figure 1	Perimeter of Figure 2

Two numbered cubes, each numbered 1-6, are rolled. The numbers that land face up are then added together.

Column A	Column B
28. The probability that the sum will be 3	The probability that the sum will be 4

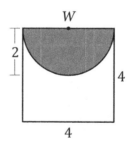

The shaded region is part of a circle that has W as its center.

Column A	Column B
29. Area of the shaded region	$\dfrac{1}{4}$ the area of the square

CONTINUE TO THE NEXT PAGE

A poll was taken to predict which of two candidates would win an election. Samples of voters were polled in two different towns. The table below shows the percent of voters surveyed in each town as well as how many voters chose each candidate.

	Town 1	Town 2
Percent of voters surveyed	10%	50%
Votes for Candidate A	36	82
Votes for Candidate B	42	14

	Column A	**Column B**
30.	Votes predicted for Candidate A in both towns	Votes predicted for Candidate B in both towns

	Column A	**Column B**
31.	$-x^2$	$(-x)^2$

Twenty four cards labeled 1-24 are put into a bag.

	Column A	**Column B**
32.	Probability of drawing a card that is a factor of 24	Probability of drawing a card that is a factor of 18

$$m > -3$$
$$n > 150$$

	Column A	**Column B**
33.	$m + 1$	$n - 2$

CONTINUE TO THE NEXT PAGE

Victoria walked 5 blocks in 3 minutes.

Charles walked 7 blocks in 4 minutes.

<u>Column A</u>	<u>Column B</u>
34. Average number of blocks that Victoria walked in one minute	Average number of blocks that Charles walked in one minute

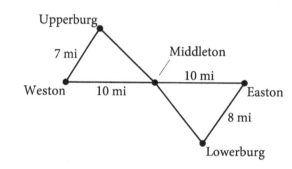

<u>Column A</u>	<u>Column B</u>
35. Distance from Lowerburg to Middleton	Distance from Upperburg to Middleton

<u>Column A</u>	<u>Column B</u>
36. $345 + 238 + 412$	$230 + 420 + 345$

<u>Column A</u>	<u>Column B</u>
37. $3y + 7$	$3y + 8$

STOP

IF YOU HAVE TIME LEFT YOU MAY CHECK YOUR ANSWERS IN THIS SECTION ONLY

Reading Comprehension

36 questions

35 minutes

The Reading Comprehension section has six short passages. Each passage has six questions after it. Choose the answer choice that comes closest to what is stated or implied in the passage. You can write in the test booklet.

STOP

DO NOT MOVE ON TO THE SECTION UNTIL TOLD TO

Questions 1-6

1   Jacqueline Cochran, one of the first female pilots in the United States, was born as
2 Bessie Lee Pittman in the Florida Panhandle. She trained as a hairdresser, changed her
3 name, and made her way to New York City. She was charming and had a winning
4 personality that she used to her advantage. She was working in the salon at the
5 prestigious Saks Fifth Avenue when a friend offered her a ride in an airplane. She was
6 hooked and began to take flying lessons at Roosevelt Field on Long Island. Within two
7 years, she had obtained her commercial pilot license.

8   In the 1930s, she developed a line of cosmetics named *Wings* and flew around the
9 country promoting her products. She also competed in flying races and in 1937 she set
10 a new record for women's flying speed.

11   By the time that World War II descended, Jacqueline Cochran was considered the
12 best female flying ace in the world. Before the United States entered World War II,
13 Cochran joined a group called "Wings for Britain". While the United States had not
14 officially joined the war, they were supplying American-built aircraft to their allies in
15 Britain and these aircraft needed to be delivered across the Atlantic Ocean. When
16 Cochran flew a Lockheed Hudson V to Britain she became the first woman to fly a
17 bomber across the Atlantic Ocean. Once there, she offered her services to the Royal Air
18 Force. She worked at the British Air Transport Auxiliary (ATA) recruiting female
19 American pilots to join the war effort with the ATA.

20   In 1940, Cochran started to campaign for female pilots to be employed in the
21 United States Army Air Force. While she did not suggest that female pilots should be
22 enlisted for combat missions, she did push for them to be used to ferry aircraft to where
23 they would be needed. In 1943, the Women's Airforce Service Pilots was formed with
24 Cochran as its director. She eventually was awarded both the Distinguished Flying
25 Cross and the Distinguished Service Medal for her contributions to the American
26 military.

27   After World War II ended, Cochran continued to live an extraordinary life. She
28 became a journalist and witnessed Japanese General Yamashita surrendering in the
29 Philippines and was the first American woman to visit Japan after the war. She also
30 attended the Nuremberg Trials for war criminals. She ran for Congress in California
31 and won the Republican nomination. In the general election she narrowly lost to the
32 Democratic candidate, however, which was one of the few failures in her life. She also
33 continued to set records as a female pilot. She had come a long way from her beginnings
34 as Bessie Lee Pittman.

CONTINUE TO THE NEXT PAGE

1. Which statement best describes the main idea of the passage?

    (A) Jacqueline Cochran always knew she wanted to be a pilot.
    (B) Jacqueline Cochran was born Bessie Lee Pittman.
    (C) Jacqueline Cochran flew combat missions during World War II.
    (D) Jacqueline Cochran lived a remarkable life.

2. This passage states that Jacqueline Cochran had a personality that was

    (A) appealing.
    (B) curious.
    (C) sullen.
    (D) unruly.

3. According to the passage, before World War II Jacqueline Cochran used her flying skills to

    (A) transport military planes.
    (B) promote her cosmetics brand.
    (C) run for the United States congress.
    (D) travel to Japan.

4. The passage provides evidence for which statement?

    (A) Jacqueline Cochran was the first female flying ace.
    (B) The United States did not have bombers to send to Britain.
    (C) Britain entered World War II before the United States did.
    (D) Jacqueline Cochran grew up in California.

5. It can be inferred from the passage that

    (A) female pilots were not allowed on combat missions during World War II.
    (B) Bessie Lee Pittman was a fantastic hairdresser.
    (C) pilot licenses were easy to obtain in the 1930s.
    (D) the Royal Air Force did not accept female pilots.

6. Which statement best describes how this passage is organized?

    (A) Two opposing opinions are presented and then debated.
    (B) Several opinions are followed by a conclusion.
    (C) Facts are presented in chronological order.
    (D) Specific facts are followed by broad generalizations.

CONTINUE TO THE NEXT PAGE

Questions 7-12

1   As humans travel through life, there are many situations in which their behavior

2 does not match their beliefs. For example, a doctor who knows very well the damage

3 that smoking cigarettes causes may still choose to smoke. Psychologists have labeled

4 this phenomenon "cognitive dissonance".

5   There are a couple of factors that affect the level of cognitive dissonance that a

6 person feels. The first factor is how important the belief is to that person. For example,

7 maybe someone knows that it is more environmentally friendly to carry water in a

8 reusable bottle than to buy water in single-use bottles. If he doesn't think that it is all

9 that important to not buy single-use bottles, then he will not experience much cognitive

10 dissonance when he does that. However, if that person cares very passionately about

11 not using bottles that could wind up in a landfill after one use, then he will experience

12 great cognitive dissonance if he buys one.

13   Cognitive dissonance can also be affected by how far a behavior strays from a

14 person's beliefs. For instance, maybe a person does not eat pork for religious reasons.

15 If this person consumes food that was prepared in a kitchen that might have had pork

16 in it at some point, then she would feel less dissonance than if she were to eat a pork

17 chop.

18   Cognitive dissonance is an uncomfortable feeling and many people use different

19 strategies in order to reduce their own level of dissonance. One strategy is to change

20 their actions. The doctor could stop smoking and the cognitive dissonance would

21 disappear. Another strategy is to justify the behavior. In our example above with the

22 single use water bottles, that person might tell himself that just using that kind of water

23 bottle once will not have a great effect on the environment one way or another. Perhaps

24 the simplest strategy to reduce cognitive dissonance is just to deny the information that

25 conflicts with the belief. In the pork example, that person might just pretend that she

26 didn't know the dinner was made from pork. While it is simple to use denial as a way

27 to reduce dissonance, it is not always easy. It would be tough for a person to convince

28 herself that pork was not in fact pork. Similarly, it would also be hard for a doctor to

29 deny either that he was smoking a cigarette or that cigarettes harm health.

30   Every person experiences cognitive dissonance at some point in his or her life and

31 it goes by many other names. Part of being human is to be confronted with our own

32 actions that sometimes do not completely match our beliefs.

CONTINUE TO THE NEXT PAGE

7. The author would most likely agree with which statement about cognitive dissonance?

    (A) It can be avoided altogether.
    (B) There is no way to reduce the cognitive dissonance that a person feels.
    (C) It is not well understood.
    (D) Experiencing it is part of being human.

8. In line 21, the word "justify" comes closest in meaning to

    (A) applaud.
    (B) pardon.
    (C) satisfy.
    (D) train.

9. According to the passage, which situation would cause cognitive dissonance?

    (A) A vegetarian eats a steak.
    (B) An athlete goes for a run.
    (C) A nurse signs up for a dance class.
    (D) A principal attends classes.

10. The main point of the third paragraph (lines 13-17) is that cognitive dissonance

    (A) only happens to people who are in a group.
    (B) is easily avoidable.
    (C) is affected by the difference between a person's beliefs and their actions.
    (D) cannot be defined in certain terms.

11. The passage provides evidence to support which statement?

    (A) Single use water bottles are harmful to the environment.
    (B) Cognitive dissonance tends to be reduced as a person gets older.
    (C) Psychologists do not have solid evidence for the existence of cognitive dissonance.
    (D) Cognitive dissonance is limited in everyday interactions.

12. How is the passage as a whole organized?

    (A) An argument is introduced and evidence for both sides is presented.
    (B) Concepts are introduced and illustrations are provided.
    (C) A controversial opinion is presented and defended vigorously.
    (D) A series of opinions are followed by a conclusion.

CONTINUE TO THE NEXT PAGE

Questions 13-18

1   Throughout history, species have been imported in to new locations for various
2 reasons. These species then find themselves in a habitat that often has no natural
3 predators. Their populations can quickly explode and government agencies and
4 environmental groups scramble to respond. Once a species has found a new home,
5 however, it can be almost impossible to extract.

6   One example of such an invasive species is the nutria rodent, which has taken over
7 whole swaths of Southeastern Louisiana. Nutria were first introduced into the marshes
8 of Louisiana in the 1930s from fur farms. It is not clear whether releasing them into the
9 wild was intentional, but initially the rodents were considered a positive element. They
10 lived in the marshes and ate what were considered aquatic "weeds", such as the water
11 hyacinth, which is known for choking out other plants.

12   By the 1950s, however, the nutria population had exploded and reports of
13 widespread damage were coming in. Complaints were received from rice and sugarcane
14 farmers that the nutria were destroying their valuable crops. Natural levees, which were
15 groups of plants that held back storm waters, were being completely denuded by the
16 hungry nutria, leaving the marshes more vulnerable to damage from major storms.
17 Nutria were no longer considered a benefit to the marsh and they were removed from
18 the list of protected wildlife.

19   The nutria could now be hunted for their pelts. Between 1962 and 1982, 1.3 million
20 nutria were killed for their furs. Reports of damage from the nutria began to decline as
21 the nutria population shrank and the ecosystems began to rebound. The respite from
22 nutria damage proved to be short lived, however. In the mid-1980s, fur became less and
23 less popular. As the demand for fur shrank, fewer nutria were hunted and their
24 population was able to grow again.

25   Another haunting story is that of the Asian carp. Just like the nutria, Asian carp
26 were initially seen as a benefit. They were imported to the southern United States in
27 order to keep retention ponds for wastewater and aquaculture operations clean. When
28 these ponds flooded, the fish were accidentally released into the Mississippi River and
29 have since spread up the Mississippi, Missouri, and Illinois rivers. The Asian carp eat
30 the same food as native species, and have no local predators, so they are rapidly
31 destroying many other plant and fish species along these rivers. The race is on to keep
32 these fish from entering into the Great Lakes and causing damage there as well.

33   Nature is a delicate balance, as the history of the nutria and the Asian carp has
34 shown. Once a species has been released into a habitat with no natural predators, the
35 damage can be devastating. Stricter laws and greater enforcement need to be enacted
36 because once a plant or animal has been released, that action can almost never be taken
37 back.

CONTINUE TO THE NEXT PAGE

13. The main idea of this passage is that invasive species

(A) are a natural part of an ecosystem.
(B) provide much needed predators to an area.
(C) are not known to exist in the United States.
(D) are difficult to control and cause harm to ecosystems.

14. Which statement about nutria can be supported by the passage?

(A) Nutria were introduced in Louisiana by sugarcane farmers.
(B) Nutria grow and reproduce quickly.
(C) Nutria were initially viewed positively in Louisiana.
(D) Nutria can be wiped out by a major storm.

15. According to the passage, how do Asian carp affect other fish populations?

(A) Asian carp eat the food in an area and other fish populations are reduced.
(B) Asian carp provide prey for other fish species and their numbers increase.
(C) Asian carp reduce plant populations but other fish species are unaffected.
(D) Asian carp eat larger fish species so that species' numbers are reduced.

16. In line 5, the word "extract" comes closest in meaning to

(A) flatter.
(B) hoist.
(C) plan.
(D) remove.

17. Which statement best describes the population growth of the nutria in Southeastern Louisiana as described in the passage?

(A) It has steadily increased from the 1920s to now.
(B) It rises and falls depending on the demand for fur.
(C) It was booming in the 1950s but is now dramatically lower.
(D) It has remained unchanged since the nutria were introduced.

18. How is this passage organized?

(A) An argument is presented and then examples are provided that support this argument.
(B) A hypothesis is explained followed by a description of how it could be tested.
(C) Two opposing theories are presented and debated.
(D) Opinions and facts are alternately presented.

CONTINUE TO THE NEXT PAGE

Questions 19-24

1   In San Jose, California, there exists an extraordinary home filled with oddities
2   called "The Winchester Mystery House". There are stairways that lead nowhere, doors
3   that open into walls, and the house sprawls over 6 acres, which is about the size of six
4   football fields. It has windows that open not to the outside but rather to a staircase that
5   leads up and then back down to the same level. There are columns that are installed
6   upside down and secret passageways that open in the middle of walls.

7   This home was built by the eccentric Sarah Winchester. Sarah Winchester was
8   born Sarah Pardee in New Haven, CT, as the daughter of a wealthy carriage
9   manufacturer. She married William Wirt Winchester, who was a member of the family
10   that produced the Winchester Repeating Rifle, known as the gun that tamed the west.
11   Its use was widespread during the American Civil war and it created a tremendous
12   fortune for the Winchester family. Sarah and William moved in the highest social
13   circles in New England. When William passed away from tuberculosis, however, Sarah
14   was absolutely devastated. She went to Boston to consult with a medium about how to
15   deal with her immense grief.

16   According to legend, the medium told Sarah that spirits of the people killed by the
17   Winchester Rifle were haunting the fortune that she had inherited when her husband
18   passed away. Supposedly, the medium told Sarah that the only way to appease the spirits
19   was to move west and build a home for them. As long as the home was never completed,
20   Sarah would be safe from the spirits.

21   Sarah went to California and found the perfect piece of land in the Santa Clara
22   Valley for her new home. For the next thirty-six years Sarah had workers building her
23   home twenty-four hours a day. There were no blueprints used. She would just meet
24   with her foreman, John Hansen, in the morning and sketch out what she wanted. There
25   were 160 rooms that she added haphazardly, forty-seven fireplaces, and seventeen
26   chimneys.

27   It is said that some of the oddities of the home were due to Ms. Winchester trying
28   to evade the spirits. The secret passageways and sharp twists and turns were to allow
29   Ms. Winchester to slip away from the ghosts that followed her, according to legend.
30   One theory is that the upside down columns were meant to confuse and disorient any
31   haunted beings that were trying to navigate the home. Other features of the home were
32   explained as practical concerns. For example, the Switchback Stairway has seven flights
33   and forty-four stairs but only manages to rise nine feet. Each step is only two inches
34   high, perhaps because Ms. Winchester suffered from severe arthritis and higher steps
35   made her joints hurt.

36   We will never know the reasons behind Ms. Winchester's unusual decisions – the
37   woman was as private as she was eccentric.

CONTINUE TO THE NEXT PAGE

19. Which statement about Sarah Winchester would the author most likely agree with?

    (A) It is certain that she built the home to confuse the spirits that haunted her.
    (B) She moved from California to New Haven to build her home.
    (C) She supervised the construction of a home with many peculiar features.
    (D) Her money was depleted before the project was completed.

20. In line 18, the word "supposedly" is used in order to let the reader know that

    (A) the next statement contradicts an earlier point.
    (B) the following statement is not a confirmed fact.
    (C) the writer personally heard the story from Sarah Winchester.
    (D) the medium was unsure of what she was saying.

21. According to the passage, the Switchback Stairway was built for the purpose of

    (A) confusing spirits.
    (B) keeping the house warmer.
    (C) creating work to keep the project going.
    (D) reducing Sarah Winchester's physical discomfort.

22. Which word best describes the Winchester Mystery House as described in the passage?

    (A) disorderly
    (B) honorable
    (C) poised
    (D) useful

23. According to the passage, why was construction performed on the home twenty-four hours a day?

    (A) It was a complex project that would have taken too long to build with breaks.
    (B) Sarah Winchester wanted the project completed quickly.
    (C) A medium told Sarah Winchester she would be safe as long as the home was not completed.
    (D) Sarah Winchester frequently changed her mind about what she wanted.

24. How is this passage organized?

    (A) A problem is presented with a series of possible solutions.
    (B) A concept is introduced and then partially explained.
    (C) A common misconception is stated and then corrected.
    (D) A series of unrelated facts are given.

CONTINUE TO THE NEXT PAGE

Questions 25-30

1   Harvesting crops in the farm fields of the American West is back-breaking work

2 with little monetary reward. The job has little to recommend it – families have to move

3 frequently to follow the crops that need harvesting, bad weather can destroy income,

4 and there is little stability. This role is often filled by recent immigrants who do not

5 have the language skills and education that would be required for many other jobs.

6   In the early 1900s, there were several attempts to organize farmworkers so that they

7 could demand better pay and working conditions from growers. None of them were

8 very successful because it was easy for growers to replace workers who made demands.

9 At one point, it was even illegal for workers to organize. There was a glimmer of hope

10 in 1936 with the passage of the National Labor Relations Act that allowed employees to

11 form unions. Unfortunately, in order to get the law passed, farm workers were explicitly

12 left out of this protection.

13   Cesar Chavez thought there must be a different way. In the early 1960s, he used

14 the model of community organization to help farmworkers. Chavez and his associates

15 travelled up and down California's agricultural region talking to workers. They asked

16 how they could help people, held house meetings, and invited them to join their

17 organization, the National Farmworkers' Association (NFWA). Chavez taught

18 nonviolence to workers as they fought for better working conditions.

19   It was slow going, up until September 8, 1965. On this day, another farmworker's

20 group called Agricultural Worker's Organizing Committee (AWOC) declared a strike

21 on the Delano table grape growers. A week later, the NFWA joined the AWOC, and

22 eventually the two groups would merge to become the United Farmworkers Organizing

23 Committee (UFWOC).

24   This strike captured the attention of the American public. It was a classic David

25 versus Goliath struggle where the powerful grape growers attempted to deny the

26 requests of the powerless farm workers. The farm workers went on strike, refusing to

27 pick the grapes of the Delano farmers. When the Delano farmers employed other

28 workers to harvest the grapes, the striking workers got the longshoremen to refuse to

29 load the grapes onto ships, leaving tons of grapes worthlessly rotting on the docks in

30 Oakland. The UFWOC even appealed directly to American consumers, encouraging

31 them not to buy grapes produced by the Delano Farmers.

32   It was a long journey, but in 1969, the Delano farmers signed an agreement with

33 the UFWOC. The workers would be paid higher wages, protected from the dangerous

34 chemicals used in agriculture, and medical clinics would be provided for farm workers.

CONTINUE TO THE NEXT PAGE

25. The primary purpose of this passage is to

    (A) convince the reader to take a particular action.
    (B) provide a comprehensive history of farmworkers.
    (C) imply that Delano growers were treated unfairly.
    (D) share the history of one group's struggle.

26. It can be inferred from the passage that a "David versus Goliath" (lines 24-25) struggle occurs when

    (A) a weak opponent confronts a much stronger one.
    (B) two opponents are equally matched.
    (C) no weapons are used.
    (D) there is no clear winner.

27. The passage implies that longshoremen

    (A) supported the Delano grape growers.
    (B) did not possess any real power in labor disputes.
    (C) were responsible for loading produce onto departing ships.
    (D) lacked their own labor union.

28. The author would most likely agree with which statement about Cesar Chavez?

    (A) He quickly gave up on the grape strike when it was unsuccessful.
    (B) He built relationships with many farmworkers as a method of organizing them.
    (C) He encouraged farmworkers to use the threat of physical harm.
    (D) He had close ties with both the farmworkers and the grape growers.

29. The author's tone when discussing Cesar Chavez can best be described as

    (A) admiring.
    (B) disapproving.
    (C) playful.
    (D) tense.

30. Which statement can be supported with evidence from the passage?

    (A) The strike left the growers without workers to pick the crops.
    (B) The National Labor Relations Act provided a better life for farmworkers.
    (C) The AWOC resisted joining with other groups.
    (D) The farmworkers achieved the goal of better treatment although it was a long process.

CONTINUE TO THE NEXT PAGE

Questions 31-36

1   Next time you are walking down the street and smell the clearly recognizable odor
2   of French fries, it may not be a restaurant you are smelling. It could be a car driving
3   next to you. Every year restaurants throw away about 100 million gallons of used
4   vegetable oil, often paying another company to properly dispose of it for them.

5   There is another option, however. Some enterprising souls have converted their
6   diesel engine cars to burn used restaurant oil. Restaurant owners are often happy to
7   have these drivers pick up their used oil for free rather than having to pay to have it
8   taken away. The drivers can then use this free oil to power their vehicle after they install
9   a simple conversion kit.

10   Before it can be used in a diesel vehicle, the oil must first be filtered to remove any
11   food particles that remain. The vehicle must also have an added fuel tank with a heating
12   element. The fuel must be kept hot in order for it to burn, unlike ordinary diesel fuel.
13   A dedicated fuel line then delivers the filtered vegetable oil to the engine.

14   Recycling vegetable oil is not likely to become a widespread practice. There is
15   simply not enough oil produced at restaurants to run very many cars. For this reason,
16   it is not likely to make a great impact on the environment. For the people who are
17   willing to go through the hassle of converting their vehicle, regularly picking up oil from
18   restaurants, and then filtering that oil, a lot of money can be saved. With diesel fuel
19   regularly running over $3 a gallon, there are significant savings to be realized. There is
20   one important caveat, however. The car will often wind up smelling like the food that
21   was cooked in it. Drivers looking to convert their own engines should think carefully
22   about how they feel about smelling like French fries versus egg rolls.

CONTINUE TO THE NEXT PAGE

31. Which statement best expresses one of the main points of this passage?

    (A) Many restaurants turn a nice profit from donating vegetable oil.
    (B) Only diesel engines can use recycled oil.
    (C) Recycled oil from restaurants takes work but can save money for drivers.
    (D) Reusing restaurant oil is a potential solution for improving the environment.

32. French fries and egg rolls are provided as examples of

    (A) foods that are easily found in restaurants.
    (B) foods that can be cooked in vegetable oil at restaurants.
    (C) the variety of food available in the United States.
    (D) a limited resource.

33. According to the passage, why must a car converted to run on vegetable oil have a fuel tank added to it?

    (A) Vegetable oil must be heated but regular diesel gasoline does not.
    (B) A vehicle that runs on vegetable oil burns more fuel so a backup tank is needed.
    (C) A converted car needs to mix diesel with vegetable oil.
    (D) It is hard to pour vegetable oil into a standard fuel tank.

34. Which of the following is implied about diesel engines in the passage?

    (A) They are not commonly used in cars.
    (B) They can only use diesel fuel.
    (C) Any food particles in the fuel would damage the engine.
    (D) They use less fuel than other types of engines.

35. The phrase "enterprising souls" in line 5 refers to people

    (A) who run restaurants.
    (B) who developed conversion kits for diesel engines.
    (C) in charge of building new cars.
    (D) willing to experiment with a process.

36. How is this passage organized?

    (A) Several competing theories are proposed and the evidence for each theory is weighed.
    (B) A concept is presented and then the advantages and disadvantages are discussed.
    (C) Two conflicting viewpoints are explained and one is proven correct.
    (D) A series of opinions are stated.

STOP

IF YOU HAVE TIME LEFT YOU MAY CHECK YOUR ANSWERS IN THIS SECTION ONLY

Mathematics Achievement

47 questions
40 minutes

Each math question has four answer choices after it. Choose the answer choice that best answers the question.

Make sure that you fill in the correct answer on your answer sheet. You may write in the test booklet.

SAMPLE QUESTION:

1. Which number can be divided by 4 with nothing left over?

   (A) 6
   ● 12
   (C) 15
   (D) 22

Since 12 can be divided by 4 with no remainder, circle B is filled in.

STOP

DO NOT MOVE ON TO THE SECTION UNTIL TOLD TO

1. What is the greatest common factor of 72 and 84?

    (A) 2
    (B) 6
    (C) 12
    (D) 6,084

2. During a party, $\frac{5}{8}$ of a birthday cake was eaten. The following day, $\frac{1}{2}$ of the cake that remained was eaten. What fraction of the cake was left?

    (A) $\frac{3}{16}$
    (B) $\frac{3}{8}$
    (C) $\frac{6}{10}$
    (D) $\frac{5}{8}$

3. A bus rental company charges $50 for the first three miles of a trip and $2 for each mile after the first three miles. Which equation would allow a person to figure out the cost, C, of renting a bus for a trip that is m miles long?

    (A) $C = 50 + 2m$
    (B) $C = 50m + 2(m - 1)$
    (C) $C = 50 + 2(m - 1)$
    (D) $C = 50 + 2(m - 3)$

4. In the equation $\frac{x + 4}{x} = \frac{6}{10}$, what is the value of x?

    (A) 10
    (B) 6
    (C) −4
    (D) −10

CONTINUE TO THE NEXT PAGE

5. If the area of a square is 49 cm², then what is its perimeter?

   (A) 7 cm²
   (B) 28 cm²
   (C) 49 cm²
   (D) 196 cm²

6. The expression $\dfrac{80(46 + 54)}{4}$ is equivalent to

   (A) 1,080
   (B) 1,840
   (C) 2,000
   (D) 8,000

7. In a box there are yellow and red sticks. There are 6 more red sticks than yellow sticks. If there are 10 yellow sticks, then what fraction of the sticks are red?

   (A) $\dfrac{3}{8}$

   (B) $\dfrac{3}{5}$

   (C) $\dfrac{8}{13}$

   (D) $\dfrac{5}{8}$

8. Pauline is drawing a map of a campground. The scale of her map is 2 centimeters equals 150 feet. If two campsites are 375 feet apart, how far apart should they be on Pauline's map?

   (A) 5 cm
   (B) 7 cm
   (C) 10 cm
   (D) 75 cm

CONTINUE TO THE NEXT PAGE

9. Today the number of swimmers in the pool increased by two and half times the number of swimmers in the pool yesterday. By what percent did the number of swimmers increase?

    (A) 100%
    (B) 150%
    (C) 200%
    (D) 250%

10. The cost of renting a restaurant for an event, r, depends upon how many people, p, will be attending the event. The formula for figuring out the cost of renting the restaurant for an event is $r = 25p + 150$. In this formula, what does the number 150 mean?

    (A) When 0 guests come to the event, the cost is $150.
    (B) For every 25 guests at the event, the cost is $150.
    (C) For every one guest at the event, the cost is $150.
    (D) For every 150 guests at the event, the cost is $25.

11. The scatterplot below shows the cost of land sold in one town during the last year.

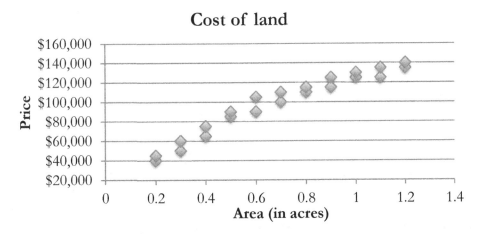

According to the scatterplot, about how much would it cost to purchase land that was 0.6 acres in size?

    (A) $80,000
    (B) $100,000
    (C) $120,000
    (D) $140,000

CONTINUE TO THE NEXT PAGE

12. A spinner has equal sections labeled 1-3, as shown below.

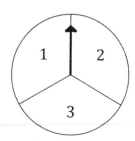

If it will be spun twice, which of the following would describe complementary events?

(A) The spinner lands on 2 and then lands on 3.

(B) The spinner lands on 3 and then lands on 3 again.

(C) The spinner lands on 1 and then lands on 2 or 3.

(D) The spinner lands on 1 and then lands on 1 or 2.

13. In the equation $2\dfrac{2}{3} \div m = \dfrac{16}{21}$, what is the value of m?

(A) $\dfrac{2}{7}$

(B) $1\dfrac{1}{3}$

(C) $2\dfrac{2}{7}$

(D) $3\dfrac{1}{2}$

14. The cost of wood flooring is $3.60 per square foot installed. How much would it cost to have wood flooring installed in a room that is 12 feet by 20 feet?

(A) $720

(B) $864

(C) $960

(D) $1,040

CONTINUE TO THE NEXT PAGE

15. Hector has 5 baseball hats, only one of which is red. He also has 4 baseball shirts, only one of which is red. He has 8 pairs of baseball socks, only one of which is red. If he randomly chooses one hat, one baseball shirt, and one pair of baseball socks, what is the probability that they will all be red?

   (A) $\dfrac{1}{160}$

   (B) $\dfrac{1}{32}$

   (C) $\dfrac{1}{20}$

   (D) $\dfrac{23}{40}$

16. What is the slope of a line that goes through the points $(4, -2)$ and $(-3, 7)$?

   (A) $\dfrac{9}{7}$

   (B) $\dfrac{7}{9}$

   (C) $-\dfrac{7}{9}$

   (D) $-\dfrac{9}{7}$

17. What is the value of B in the equation $\dfrac{B}{36} = \dfrac{24}{32}$?

   (A) 8

   (B) 25

   (C) 27

   (D) 30

18. Which of the following multiplication problems would have 4 digits in its answer?

   (A) 11×9
   (B) 13×14
   (C) 20×51
   (D) 99×102

CONTINUE TO THE NEXT PAGE

19. Patty plotted the points $(4, 1)$, $(5, 6)$, $(4, 7)$, and $(3, 6)$ on a coordinate grid. She then connected these points to create a quadrilateral that had these points as vertices. Which term best describes the quadrilateral that she created?

    (A) kite
    (B) trapezoid
    (C) square
    (D) rectangle

20. Which expression is equivalent to $\dfrac{x}{y}\left(\dfrac{x}{w} - \dfrac{y}{w}\right)$?

    (A) $\dfrac{2x - xy}{wy}$

    (B) $\dfrac{x^2 - y}{wy}$

    (C) $\dfrac{x}{w}\left(\dfrac{x}{y} - 1\right)$

    (D) $\dfrac{x}{w}\left(1 - \dfrac{x}{y}\right)$

21. The figure below gives the first four elements in a pattern.

What is the fifth element in this pattern?

(A)

(B)

(C)

(D)

CONTINUE TO THE NEXT PAGE

22. Which number line correctly represents $y < -4$?

(A)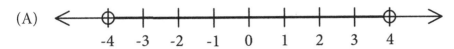

(B)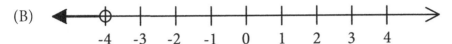

(C)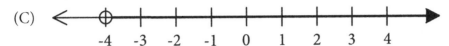

(D)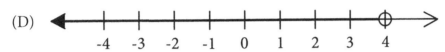

23. Use the input-output chart below to answer the question.

Input	Output
2	8
4	14
6	20
n	?

Which expression represents the output if the input is n?

(A) $n + 6$
(B) $3n - 2$
(C) $3n + 2$
(D) $4n$

24. For a school fundraiser, students sold 150 tickets to a carwash that was to be held on a Friday. On Monday, they sold 23 tickets, on Tuesdays they sold 34 tickets, on Wednesday they 13 tickets, and on Thursday they sold 48 tickets. The rest of the tickets were sold at the actual car wash. If the tickets were $3 in advance or $4 at the carwash, how much total money did the students collect?

(A) $354
(B) $450
(C) $482
(D) $600

CONTINUE TO THE NEXT PAGE

25. Pearl spent $\frac{3}{5}$ of her allowance on books and spent the remaining $4 on a snack. What is Pearl's allowance?

    (A) $10

    (B) $12

    (C) $13

    (D) $15

26. Lola had $3\frac{2}{3}$ cups of flour. She used $1\frac{3}{4}$ cups of flour to make a cake. How many cups of flour did she have left?

    (A) $1\frac{11}{12}$

    (B) $2\frac{1}{12}$

    (C) $2\frac{1}{2}$

    (D) $2\frac{3}{4}$

27. Which of the following shows 120 as the product of its prime factors?

    (A) 60×2

    (B) 40×30

    (C) $30 \times 2 \times 2$

    (D) $5 \times 3 \times 2 \times 2 \times 2$

CONTINUE TO THE NEXT PAGE

28. Use the triangle below to answer the question.

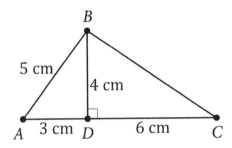

What is the area of triangle *ABC*?

(Note: area of triangle $= \frac{1}{2} \times b \times h$)

(A) 6 cm²

(B) 12 cm²

(C) 18 cm²

(D) 24 cm²

29. In which number does the digit 6 represent $\frac{6}{100}$?

(A) 3.64

(B) 4.096

(C) 5.263

(D) 600.45

30. There are red and white flowers in a bouquet. If a flower is randomly chosen, the probability that it will be white is $\frac{2}{5}$. There are 9 red flowers. How many total flowers are in the bouquet?

(A) 15

(B) 18

(C) 20

(D) 21

CONTINUE TO THE NEXT PAGE

31. Use the figure below to answer the question.

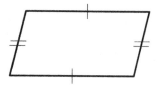

What is the best term to describe this shape?

(A) trapezoid
(B) parallelogram
(C) kite
(D) rhombus

32. What is the value of $3.15 + 2.4 + 0.6 + 0.42$?

(A) 6.15
(B) 6.32
(C) 6.47
(D) 6.57

33. The triangles below are similar.

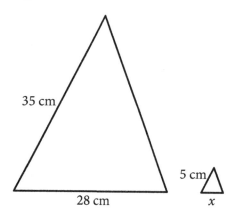

What is the value of x?

(A) 3 cm
(B) 4 cm
(C) 5 cm
(D) 7 cm

CONTINUE TO THE NEXT PAGE

34. Use the graph below to answer the question.

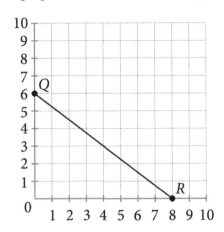

Line s (not shown) is perpendicular to $\overline{QR}$ at $(4, 3)$. What is the equation of line s?

(A) $y = \dfrac{4}{3}x - 2\dfrac{1}{3}$

(B) $y = \dfrac{4}{3}x + 2\dfrac{1}{3}$

(C) $y = -\dfrac{4}{3}x - 2\dfrac{1}{3}$

(D) $y = -\dfrac{3}{4}x - 2\dfrac{1}{3}$

35. If a number can be divided by both 3 and 4 leaving no remainder, what other number can it also be divided by with no remainder?

(A) 7

(B) 8

(C) 12

(D) 15

CONTINUE TO THE NEXT PAGE

36. The larger cube shown in Figure 1 was created by stacking the smaller cubes shown in Figure 2.

Figure 1   **Figure 2**

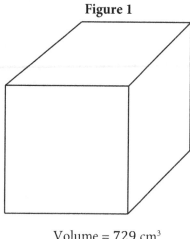

Volume = 729 cm^3 Volume = 27 cm^3

How many of the smaller cubes were used to create the large cube?

(A) 3
(B) 9
(C) 27
(D) 81

37. The sum of g and h is 18. What is the greatest possible value for the product of g and h?

(A) 72
(B) 81
(C) 88
(D) 90

38. The number 14 is 20 percent of

(A) 70
(B) 90
(C) 110
(D) 140

CONTINUE TO THE NEXT PAGE

39. Use the number set below to answer the question.

$$\{10, 6, 8, 9, 12, 4\}$$

Which of the following statements is true about these numbers?

(A) the average is equal to the median
(B) the mode is equal to the average
(C) the range is equal to the median
(D) the median is equal to 8.5

40. Which is equivalent to $3(v + w)$?

(A) $3v + w$

(B) $v + 3w$

(C) $3v + 3w$

(D) $\dfrac{v}{3} + \dfrac{w}{3}$

41. Which expression is equivalent to $\dfrac{\sqrt{16}(\sqrt{4} + 2x)}{2}$?

(A) $1 + x$
(B) $2(2 + 2x)$
(C) $2(1 + x)$
(D) $4(2 + 2x)$

42. Which is equivalent to 2.3 hours?

(A) 2 hours 3 minutes
(B) 2 hours 6 minutes
(C) 2 hours 18 minutes
(D) 2 hours 30 minutes

CONTINUE TO THE NEXT PAGE

43. On the coordinate grid below, triangle *KLM* was transformed in order to create triangle *K'L'M'*.

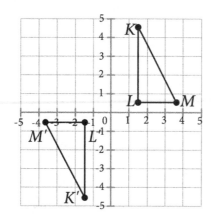

What transformation was performed?

(A) two reflections
(B) a slide
(C) a 90 degree rotation
(D) two slides

44. The graph below shows the cost per widget when different quantities of widgets are produced.

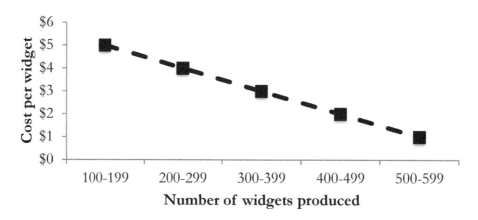

What would be the total cost if 320 widgets were produced?

(A) $3
(B) $96
(C) $640
(D) $960

CONTINUE TO THE NEXT PAGE

45. Jerry surveyed the students in his class about their favorite animals at the zoo. His data is shown in the circle graph below.

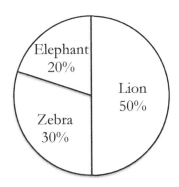

Which could have been the responses that he received in order to create this circle graph?

(A)   15 lion, 10 elephant, 10 zebra

(B)   15 lion, 10 elephant, 5 zebra

(C)   15 lion, 9 zebra, 6 elephant

(D)   15 lion, 6 zebra, 9 elephant

46. If $r - 6 + 4 = p$, then what is the vale of $p - r$?

(A) -6

(B) -2

(C)   2

(D)   6

47. Randal wants to estimate the value of the expression shown.

$$(69 \times 72) \div 600$$

Which is the best estimate?

(A)   7

(B)   8

(C)   80

(D)   90

STOP

IF YOU HAVE TIME LEFT YOU MAY CHECK YOUR ANSWERS IN THIS SECTION ONLY

Essay

You will be given 30 minutes to plan and write an essay. The topic is printed on the next page. *Make sure that you write about this topic. Do NOT choose another topic.*

This essay gives you the chance to show your thinking and how well you can express your ideas. Do not worry about filling all of the space provided. The quality is more important than how much you write. You should write more than a brief paragraph, though.

A copy of this essay will be sent to the schools that you apply to. Make sure that you only write in the appropriate area on the answer sheet. Please print so that the admissions officers can understand what you wrote.

On the next page is the topic sheet. There is room on this sheet to make notes and collect your thoughts. The final essay should be written on the two lined sheets provided in the answer sheet, however. Make sure that you copy your topic at the top of the first lined page. Write only in blue or black ink. (Answer sheets are found at the beginning of this book and you can go to www.testprepworks.com/student/download to download additional copies.)

REMINDER: Please remember to write the topic on the top of the first lined page in your answer sheet.

> If you could have one person from history over for dinner, who it would it be? What would you talk to this person about?

- Write only about this topic
- Only the lined sheets will be sent to schools
- Use only blue or black ink

Notes

_____

_____

_____

_____

_____

_____

_____

_____

_____

_____

_____

_____

_____

_____

_____

_____

_____

_____

_____

Answers

Verbal Reasoning Answers

Correct answer	Your answer	Put a checkmark here if you answered the question correctly
1. C		
2. D		
3. B		
4. A		
5. B		
6. C		
7. D		
8. D		
9. A		
10. B		
11. C		
12. A		
13. B		
14. C		
15. A		
16. A		
17. C		
18. B		

19. A		
20. C		
21. D		
22. C		
23. B		
24. A		
25. B		
26. D		
27. C		
28. B		
29. C		
30. A		
31. D		
32. A		
33. B		
34. C		
35. D		
36. C		
37. D		
38. A		
39. A		
40. B		
Total questions answered correctly: _____		

Interpreting Your Verbal Reasoning Score

On the ISEE, your raw score is the number of questions that you answered correctly on each section. Nothing is subtracted for the questions that you answered incorrectly.

Your raw score is then converted into a scaled score. This scaled score is then converted into a percentile score. Remember that it is the percentile score that schools are looking at. Your percentile score compares you just to other students in your grade.

Below is a chart that gives a very rough conversion between your raw score on the practice Verbal Reasoning section and a percentile score.

PLEASE NOTE – The purpose of this chart is to let you see how the scoring works, not to give you an accurate percentile score. You will need to complete the official practice test in *What to Expect on the ISEE*, available for download from ERB at www.erblearn.org, in order to get a more accurate percentile score.

Middle Level Verbal Reasoning

Applicants to Grade 7			
Percentile score	25th	50th	75th
Approximate raw score needed	19-20	25-26	29-30

Applicants to Grade 8			
Percentile score	25th	50th	75th
Approximate raw score needed	24-25	28-29	32-33

Quantitative Reasoning Answers

Correct answer	Your answer	Put a checkmark here if you answered the question correctly
1. D		
2. B		
3. B		
4. B		
5. C		
6. C		
7. D		
8. A		
9. D		
10. C		
11. B		
12. C		
13. A		
14. C		
15. B		
16. A		
17. C		
18. D		
19. D		
20. A		
21. B		

22. B		
23. C		
24. B		
25. A		
26. D		
27. C		
28. B		
29. A		
30. A		
31. D		
32. A		
33. D		
34. B		
35. D		
36. C		
37. B		
Total questions answered correctly: _____		

Interpreting Your Quantitative Reasoning Score

On the ISEE, your raw score is the number of questions that you answered correctly on each section. Nothing is subtracted for the questions that you answered incorrectly.

Your raw score is then converted into a scaled score. This scaled score is then converted into a percentile score. Remember that it is the percentile score that schools are looking at. Your percentile score compares you just to other students in your grade.

Below is a chart that gives a very rough conversion between your raw score on the practice Quantitative Reasoning section and a percentile score.

PLEASE NOTE – The purpose of this chart is to let you see how the scoring works, not to give you an accurate percentile score. You will need to complete the official practice test in *What to Expect on the ISEE*, available for download from ERB at www.erblearn.org, in order to get a more accurate percentile score.

Middle Level Quantitative Reasoning

Applicants to Grade 7			
Percentile score	25th	50th	75th
Approximate raw score needed	16-17	20-21	24-25

Applicants to Grade 8			
Percentile score	25th	50th	75th
Approximate raw score needed	20-21	23-24	26-27

Reading Comprehension Answers

Correct answer	Your answer	Put a checkmark here if you answered the question correctly
1. D		
2. A		
3. B		
4. C		
5. A		
6. C		
7. D		
8. B		
9. A		
10. C		
11. A		
12. B		
13. D		
14. C		
15. A		
16. D		
17. B		
18. A		
19. C		
20. B		
21. D		
22. A		
23. C		
24. B		

25. D		
26. A		
27. C		
28. B		
29. A		
30. D		
31. C		
32. B		
33. A		
34. C		
35. D		
36. B		
Total questions answered correctly: _____		

Interpreting Your Reading Comprehension Score

On the ISEE, your raw score is the number of questions that you answered correctly on each section. Nothing is subtracted for the questions that you answered incorrectly.

Your raw score is then converted into a scaled score. This scaled score is then converted into a percentile score. Remember that it is the percentile score that schools are looking at. Your percentile score compares you just to other students in your grade.

Below is a chart that gives a very rough conversion between your raw score on the practice Reading Comprehension section and a percentile score.

PLEASE NOTE – The purpose of this chart is to let you see how the scoring works, not to give you an accurate percentile score. You will need to complete the official practice test in *What to Expect on the ISEE*, available for download from ERB at www.erblearn.org, in order to get a more accurate percentile score.

Middle Level Reading Comprehension

Applicants to Grade 7			
Percentile score	25th	50th	75th
Approximate raw score needed	11-12	17-18	22-23

Applicants to Grade 8			
Percentile score	25th	50th	75th
Approximate raw score needed	16-17	21-22	25-26

Mathematics Achievement Answers

Correct answer	Your answer	Put a checkmark here if you answered the question correctly
1. C		
2. A		
3. D		
4. D		
5. B		
6. C		
7. C		
8. A		
9. D		
10. A		
11. B		
12. C		
13. D		
14. B		
15. A		
16. D		
17. C		
18. C		
19. A		
20. C		
21. D		
22. B		
23. C		
24. C		

25. A		
26. A		
27. D		
28. C		
29. C		
30. A		
31. B		
32. D		
33. B		
34. A		
35. C		
36. C		
37. B		
38. A		
39. D		
40. C		
41. B		
42. C		
43. A		
44. D		
45. C		
46. B		
47. B		
Total questions answered correctly: _____		

Interpreting Your Mathematics Achievement Score

On the ISEE, your raw score is the number of questions that you answered correctly on each section. Nothing is subtracted for the questions that you answered incorrectly.

Your raw score is then converted into a scaled score. This scaled score is then converted into a percentile score. Remember that it is the percentile score that schools are looking at. Your percentile score compares you just to other students in your grade.

Below is a chart that gives a very rough conversion between your raw score on the practice Mathematics Achievement section and a percentile score.

PLEASE NOTE – The purpose of this chart is to let you see how the scoring works, not to give you an accurate percentile score. You will need to complete the official practice test in *What to Expect on the ISEE*, available for download from ERB at www.erblearn.org, in order to get a more accurate percentile score.

Middle Level Mathematics Achievement

Applicants to Grade 7			
Percentile score	25th	50th	75th
Approximate raw score needed	32-33	37-38	42-43

Applicants to Grade 8			
Percentile score	25th	50th	75th
Approximate raw score needed	35-36	39-40	43-44

Books by Test Prep Works

	Content instruction	Test-taking strategies	Practice problems	Full-length practice tests
ISEE				
Lower Level (for students applying for admission to grades 5-6)				
Success on the Lower Level ISEE	✓	✓	✓	✓ (1)
30 Days to Acing the Lower Level ISEE		✓	✓	
The Best Unofficial Practice Tests for the Lower Level ISEE				✓ (2)
Middle Level (for students applying for admission to grades 7-8)				
Success on the Middle Level ISEE	✓	✓	✓	✓ (1)
The Best Unofficial Practice Tests for the Middle Level ISEE				✓ (2)
Upper Level (for students applying for admission to grades 9-12)				
Success on the Upper Level ISEE	✓	✓	✓	✓ (1)
The Best Unofficial Practice Tests for the Upper Level ISEE				✓ (2)
SSAT				
Middle Level (for students applying for admission to grades 6-8)				
Success on the Middle Level SSAT	✓	✓	✓	
The Best Unofficial Practice Tests for the Middle Level SSAT				✓ (2)
Upper Level (for students applying for admission to grades 9-12)				
Success on the Upper Level SSAT	✓	✓	✓	✓ (1)
30 Days to Acing the Upper Level SSAT		✓	✓	
The Best Unofficial Practice Tests for the Upper Level SSAT				✓ (2)

TEST PREP WORKS, LLC

Looking for more instruction and practice?

Check out our other book for the Middle Level ISEE:

Success on the Middle Level ISEE: A Complete Course

✓ Strategies specific to each section of the test

✓ Reading and vocabulary drills

✓ In-depth math content instruction with practice sets

✓ 1 full-length practice test (different from the practice tests in *The Best Unofficial Practice Tests for the Middle Level ISEE*)

Was ***The Best Unofficial Practice Tests for the Middle Level ISEE*** helpful to you?
Please consider leaving a review with the merchant where you purchased the book.
We welcome your suggestions at *feedback@testprepworks.com*.

Made in the USA
Coppell, TX
20 October 2022